THE INTERPRETATION OF PLAINCHANT

THE INTERPRETATION OF PLAINCHANT

A Preliminary Study

By ALEC ROBERTSON, A.R.A.M.

CHAPLAIN OF WESTMINSTER CATHEDRAL

GREENWOOD PRESS, PUBLISHERS

WESTPORT, CONNECTICUT

Originally published in 1937
by Oxford University Press, London

First Greenwood Reprinting 1970

Library of Congress Catalogue Card Number 72-109831

SBN 8371-4322-5

Printed in the United States of America

'Let the chant be full of gravity; let it be neither worldly, nor too rude and poor. . . . Let it be sweet, yet without levity, and, whilst it pleases the ear, let it move the heart. It should alleviate sadness, and calm the angry spirit. It should not contradict the sense of the words, but rather enhance it. For it is no slight loss of spiritual grace to be distracted from the profit of the sense by the beauty of the chant, and to have our attention drawn to a mere vocal display, when we ought to be thinking of what is sung.'

ST BERNARD OF CLAIRVAUX (1090-1153)

CONTENTS

Chapter   *Page*

  FOREWORD   ix

 I GENERAL SURVEY   I

 II TECHNICAL POINTS   10
    (i) Notation.
    (ii) Rhythm.
    (iii) Phrasing.
    (iv) The Latin Tonic Accent and Accent Hammering.
    (v) Asterisks.
    (vi) Psalms and Antiphons.
    (vii) Hymns and Sequences.
    (viii) Approach to a High Note at a Point of Climax.
    (ix) Changes of Speed.
    (x) The Melodic Echo.
    (xi) Counsels and Warnings.

 III TYPICAL LINES OF STUDY   44

 IV THE GREGORIAN COMPOSER AT WORK   ..   55

 V THE DRAMATIC IN PLAINCHANT   63
    (i) Some examples of Dramatic Dialogues and Pictures

 VI THE DRAMATIC IN PLAINCHANT (*continued*)   74
    (ii) Word Painting.

 VII FORM   90

 VIII PLAINCHANT AND BYZANTINE ART   ..   104

  CONCLUSION   108

  SELECTED BIBLIOGRAPHY   110

  INDEX OF MUSICAL EXAMPLES   115

FOREWORD

This small book is designed primarily for Catholic choirmasters who wish to be faithful to the rulings of the *Motu Proprio*, but who find plainchant distasteful to their choirs and unpopular with the congregations of their churches; and who themselves feel lukewarm about the chant or fearful on account of its supposed complexities.

I greatly hope, also, that the book may prove of interest to all who love plainchant, irrespective of creed, and that it may perhaps come into the hands of those musicians who think of plainchant—if indeed they think of it at all—as a quaint survival of the past, a barbaric and boring kind of ululation, or as mathematical exercises in discarded modes.

Few histories of music, in their perhaps necessarily brief treatment of the subject, give the reader any idea that the plainchant melodies are living, and, for the most part, perfect works of art, perfectly adapted to their continuing purpose, and it is still possible for writers on music to offer such a false idea of the chant as this: ' its primitive undeveloped sense of key, its vague rhythm, its limited compass, together with its unharmonized or accompanied presentation are all useful peculiarities considered as a means of contrast. But if used to the exclusion of modern music its primitiveness becomes only too apparent. In its best form it is eminently suited to the traditional congregational responses and, in the psalm tones, for the chanting of the prose psalms*'.

It would be hard to find a more misleading statement. The writer appears to consider the modes as merely the two modern scales in embryo, and has, apparently, no knowledge of the basic rhythm of the chant: while in his last sentence he complacently ignores the whole of the Gradual and the Antiphonal!

I have, after some thought, made use of the square notation on the four-line stave, which alone gives a true picture of the melodies, since the book is meant primarily for practising musicians to whom the reading of such notation will present no difficulties. It may prove a nuisance at first to the uninitiated, but as Mr Arnold suggests, in his admirable book *Plainsong Accompaniment*†, one has only to ' imagine a fifth line on the top of the four-line stave and think of the square notes as being modern notation ', imagining, also, of course, a key signature. I have provided a suitable ' key signature ' and a starting note for every example as far as Chapter VI, and sections on the notation and rhythm of the chant will be found in the second chapter. (The bibliography gives particulars of an edition which actually prints the old notation with a five-line stave and a key signature, but this and other such editions only cover Sundays and the greater feasts.)

The various hints on interpretation scattered through the book are to be taken not as arbitrary but as purely suggestive. Original interpretative

---

* *Music and Religion*, by Brian Webberly. (Epworth Press, 1934.)

† *Plainsong Accompaniment*, by J. H. Arnold. (Oxford University Press, 1927.)

ix

ideas—those that are far removed from what is merely eccentric—are as rare as the dodo in most performances of music. We cling timidly to the received and the traditional. Perhaps these pages will help the choirmaster to start and to go on thinking.

It has not been possible entirely to avoid a controversial tone, much as I should have wished to do so, but I trust that ' my friends, the enemy', may find that the substance, at any rate, of many of my ideas in no way conflicts with their own, a conclusion which would please no one more than myself. At least I beg them to do me the honour of reading the book as a whole, for the ideas put forward overlap and to avoid constant repetition are not continually restated.

This small book is, indeed, the merest sketch of a big subject upon which, so far as I am aware, nothing in English and little in any other language is so far available, although many volumes have been written upon the rhythm of plainchant and palaeographic questions.

Plainchant is music, and music of all the arts is the least patient of regimentation. This is one of the dangers that threatens the chant. But the greatest evil to be combated is the lack of appreciation of that which brought the chant to birth, the generating text. One may perhaps without irreverence paraphrase St John: ' The word was made melody and dwelt among us'. But in becoming melody it did not cease to be word, and it would be ' heresy' to suggest that the melody is greater than the word which generated it.

It should be clear, therefore, that the artistic success of the interpretative ideas which I put forward depends on the degree of sensibility with which the text is studied and sung.

Ignorance of the Latin should never be an excuse to ignore the text in the mouths of a Catholic choir (or congregation) since parallel English translations are now accessible to all in the various service books published for use in this country. Such translations are provided in this book for those who have no Latin*.

It is my earnest hope that musicians may work out ideas of interpretation of the chant that will show to their indifferent congregations how beautiful, inspiring, and various an art plainchant can be; and even persuade their congregations to depart from a too long spell of dumbness and bear their rightful part in the Liturgy in accordance with the express wishes of the Popes who have legislated about the chant.

I should like, in conclusion, to express my deep gratitude to the Vicar-General of the Westminster Diocese, his lordship Bishop Butt, who, in giving me permission to undertake this work, wrote as follows: ' I am delighted with your project. As you say, the purely technical aspects of rhythm, etc., have occupied the attention of students of plainchant overmuch to the exclusion of everything else. But perhaps the magnificent work of the Solesmes monks would never have been done had they

* A. M. Scarre's *Introduction to Liturgical Latin* (St Dominic's Press, 5s. 6d.) is warmly to be recommended in this connection.

not narrowed their field. Now that it *is* done, the time is ripe for some-
one to approach the whole subject from the angle which you suggest.
I speak as one less wise, having little knowledge of the matter. But,
obviously, the text is (or should be) the inspiration of the music which
interprets it.

' An explanation of how the ancient melodies fulfil this rôle and bring
out and emphasise the meaning of the words of the liturgy, should be of
great practical value: so go ahead by all means.'

I am also most grateful to Mr Hubert J. Foss for his warm encouragement of the scheme from the start, to Mr J. H. Arnold for much
valuable help and advice, and to Messrs Desclée of Tournai for kindly
giving me permission to quote the musical examples, except where
otherwise stated, from their publications with the rhythmic signs of
Solesmes.

CHAPTER I

GENERAL SURVEY

Ecclesiastical students are taught in the schools that nothing is in the intellect that is not first in the senses, and this sound philosophical principle, peculiarly the basis of artistic appreciation, has been finely reaffirmed by Bernard Kelly in a recent remarkable article upon the nature of beauty.

' The apprehension of beauty,' he writes, ' beginning in the senses, themselves informed by the soul, their active principle, awakens the deeper, more searching activity of the mind*.'

Now the appeal of music may be to the senses alone—which is, of course, the case when it is also music without mind, whose only object is to divert and titillate—or it may pass through the senses to awaken that ' deeper, more searching activity of the mind ' which we call intellectual apprehension. But there must always remain the radio-receiver of the senses, adverted to or not, however spiritually minded and imponderable the music may be.

It is the quality of purely sensuous appeal and of mere vain display that the Church has ever dreaded to find in her religious music. The history of the *Scholae Cantorum*, the debates at the Council of Trent, the publication of the *Motu Proprio*, all go to prove that her fears that beauty might be made an end in itself, and aesthetic posturing or ingenious note-spinning take the place of religious sincerity, were only too well founded.

This attitude of the Church accounts for the losing battle that she fought for so long against secular musical influences, a battle in which, however, one piece of territory was at any rate secured from serious invasion, though not from subsequent mishandling, plainchant.

In view of the Church's declared hostility towards secular influences there is a certain irony in the fact that one can trace the whole *corpus* of modern music, ranging, as it does, through the whole gamut of the emotions, to a type of congregational singing deriving from Jewish practice, which began in a section of the Persian Church in the fourth century and then spread to the entire Orient.

' The plan was to divide the congregation into two demi-choruses, one of men, the other of women and children, each delivering a verse of the psalm. After these two deliveries, one by each choir, both united in singing the refrain.

' Sometimes this refrain was one of the ancient responses, always brief; sometimes new chants, somewhat longer, were composed. The new style was called *antiphonia*. . . .

---

* ' Passage Through Beauty.' Bernard Kelly. *Blackfriars Review*. September 1935.

' The singing of responses more or less florid (as opposed to the priest's part, literally *plain*chant) by the congregation, when taken in connection with the texts used for these responses, indicates a tendency, whether conscious or unconscious, to move towards *a purely musical expression of emotion.... The element of floridity was the agent of musical freedom* .*'

Emotion had not, indeed, to wait to come into music until that moment, but it was the deliberate organisation of the emotional appeal, finding its way painfully from mouth to pen and parchment, that opened the door into the future and provided the ground for a conflict which has ever since waged in the minds of religious men.

Fear of the sensible pleasure awakened by profane art caused St Jerome bitterly to repent his delight in the classics, and St Augustine, whose heart was melted by the ' new and haunting cadence of the Ambrosian Chant ', questioned whether religion might safely ally itself with delight so exquisite of the senses. St Bernard, releasing a flood of human emotion over the death of his brother, revelling in the sensuous imagery of the ' Song of Songs ' in his greatest sermons, would not so much as raise his eyes to the majesty of the Alps when he crossed over them!

Was Ruskin right in saying that ' no Christian whose heart is thoroughly set upon the world to come, and who is, as far as human judgment can pronounce, perfect and right before God, ever cared about art at all† '; or, one may add, if he did care, he feared just that near-sensuous element inescapably in it; or, that the work of art sufficient, perfect, in itself, would lead him away from God, in whom, sacrificing beauty, he must find Beauty?

It is just this fear which in our time troubled Gerard Manley Hopkins, unwillingly a poet, and which now troubles T. S. Eliot.

Noticing a book on T. S. Eliot in the *Observer* (September 15, 1935), Basil de Selincourt helps to give a right orientation to this unhappy and unnecessary division between natural and supernatural beauty, which has led to so much disharmony. ' The poet, I apprehend, is essentially the man to whom anything else you like may be a distraction at any time, but beauty never; to which I add that " sensuous " is a mere tautology where beauty is concerned. Of course, the word beauty is as far as possible avoided in criticism, because the desirability of the thing is assumed; but when a revulsion against beauty is admitted, the word has to come back and in its application to poetry must have its complete, that is its religious, meaning. We turn to poetry that we may find through words and on the lips of man a freshness, a felicity, an exactitude which makes those words continuous, to our sense, with the other created works, and testify that they are born of the same spirit. Keats had this in mind when he said that unless poetry came as leaves to a tree, it had better not come at all; and surely there could be no greater loss, where English thought and the English tradition are concerned,

---

* *Early History of Singing*, p. 9. W. J. Henderson. (Longmans, New York, 1921.)
† *Stones of Venice*, Vol. II, p. 95. Ruskin. (Dent.)

than the separation of poetry from religion or the suggestion that there can be, in religion itself, any ultimate authority save that which poetry provides. Our religion, to be alive, must be new made every morning; our poetry must give us not flowers only, but flowers drenched in dew. That renovation, that radiance, is just what the best English work, from Chaucer to Bridges, has given us always: and we realise from it that the poet's essential power is inspiration, what we call creation being only his transmission or reflection or divination of a brightness not his own.'

Von Hügel ' also had a pronounced dislike to a hard-and-fast line between the natural and the supernatural ', and, Mr Lester Garland tells us*, was definitely afraid of any conscious preoccupation with religious study alone. ' Secular literature is to be read, not as something which religion may possibly tolerate, or over which it may throw the aegis of a condescending patronage, but as the natural expression of, and as necessary for the comprehension of, those among man's varied thoughts, aspirations, and activities which are not specifically religious but which no religion that is not emasculated can ignore. Man is body as well as soul.'

Those who have read Von Hügel's *Letters to my Niece* will remember that he lays down a course of study which includes enough ' pagan ' classics to make St Augustine and St Jerome turn in their graves! And I am sure the student of plainchant has much to gain from an intensive study of Bach and of the great *lieder* composers†. By such a study he will improve his phrasing, his melodic line-drawing, his command over vocal colour and sense of word values, and establish an emotional mean not too far removed from that of the average man.

Without doubt Ruskin's implied division of the world into saints, who will have no truck with the arts (and are oddly moved by the theatrical and false, by Carlo Dolci and Gounod!), and sinners, all the musicians, poets, and painters, seems to us, to-day, entirely unacceptable! But it is important, and not always easy, to preserve a right balance in this matter.

' It is an incontrovertible proposition ', says Dr Guardini, ' that people who consider a work of art merely from the artistic point of view do it an injustice. Its significance as a composition can only be fully estimated when it is viewed in connection with the whole of life. A work of art is in less danger from the logician or the moral philosopher pure and simple, because they stand in no particular relation to it. Deadly destructive to the work of art, however, is the purely artistic perception of the aesthete—both word and matter being taken in the worst and most extreme sense which they have possessed since, for instance, Oscar Wilde.

---

* *The Religious Philosophy of Baron Von Hügel*, pp. 74-75. Lester Garland. (Dent, 1932.)

† As Parry says in his *Bach* (p. 563) ' the line of demarcation between the sacred and secular forms was for him not decisively drawn '.

' Still more (continues Dr Guardini) does this hold good when it is a question, not of the representation of a work of art, but of actual people, and even of that tremendous unity—the *Opus Dei*, that is the liturgy—in which the Creator-Artist, the Holy Ghost, has garnered and expressed the whole fullness of reality and of creative art. Aesthetes are everywhere looked upon as unwelcome guests, as drones and as parasites sponging on life, but nowhere are they more deserving of anger and contempt than in the sphere of sacred things. The careworn man who seeks nothing at Mass but the fulfilment of the service which he owes to his God; the busy woman who comes to be a little lightened of her burden; the many people who, barren of feeling and perceiving nothing of the beauty and splendour of word and sound which surrounds them, merely seek strength for their daily toil—all these penetrate far more deeply into the essence of the liturgy than does the connoisseur who is busy savouring the contrast between the austere beauty of a Preface and the melodiousness of a Gradual*.'

The spiritual aesthete needs, also, to be reminded that though plain-song may indeed be prayer-song, it is in the senses of its hearers first as *sound* and not as prayer: and the near-sensuous element, however much spiritualized in performance, remains—else would the music be dead. The rhythm which vitalizes the chant first moves the senses, and then the spirit; its organ of expression is primarily physical, not spiritual.

We read the classics in our day and are not led away from God; we are not seduced by the Lydian mode; we lift our eyes to the hills and rejoice: we see a world in a grain of sand and heaven in a wildflower, but do not fall into the errors of pantheism. Why then should we find religious emotion, and that most carefully ironed out, only in music intended for use in Church, all other music being regarded as profane? It is surely only an imaginary gulf which separates the one-dimensional plainchant *Sanctus* from the *Sanctus* of Bach in the B minor Mass, the *Sanctus* in Byrd's five-part Mass from the great *Adagio* of Beethoven's A minor quartet. The case of St Augustine—who served us ill on the question of original sin!—reminds us that the Manichæanism which he thought himself to have abjured is by no means dead, and will live on so long as a puritan, Protestant or Catholic, remains to trouble the world. Patmore well says that the sin of seeing good in evil is venial as compared to the sin of seeing evil in good, which is peculiarly the sin of the puritan.

Let it not be forgotten that the first thing the Church commands her priests to recite in thanksgiving upon leaving the altar after the celebration of Mass is the canticle *Benedicite, omnia opera Domini*, in which all created and, in a secondary sense, creating things, are called upon to praise the Creator.

' And the greatest of God's creations, Man, must also give thanks amongst the other things for the tenderness and sweetness of humanity—

* *The Church and the Catholic*, pp. 185-6. R. Guardini. (Sheed & Ward, 1935.)

the playfulness and exuberance of the things men make for the love of the thing, for the love of their fellow men, or for the love of God* '—the greater, surely, including the less—one tremendous, all-embracing orientation which will certainly not exclude the art of the musician.

Now this little book, a study for the larger book I hope one day to write, is written with the main idea of combating the monotonous style of singing which has in so many places overcome and obscured the many beauties of plainchant, by drawing attention to the woefully neglected question of its interpretation.

So much talk about prayer-song (the order should be song-prayer), so much unnecessary cheironomic posturing, so much repellent technical jargon, an obsession about rhythm, have obscured the fact that plainchant is first and foremost *music*—but music conditioned by the text to which it is set—to be treated and interpreted not as a thing apart, but according to the basic principles of all song-interpretation.

It therefore follows that the true interpretation of plainchant requires both literary and musical perception and can only take wings of prayer if based upon a sound technical foundation.

There are too many well-intentioned people nowadays who, having attended a summer school or two, a lecture here and there, feel themselves equipped to teach plainchant when they are without any real knowledge and love of the Liturgy, any proper musical training or spacious background of musical culture, but possess only unlimited confidence in themselves.

In their hands plainchant becomes, doubtless, a science, but it ceases to be an art, and much to be pitied are the choirs who fall into the hands of these merciless mechanics. Like the unskilful organist who makes everything that he plays upon his instrument sound alike, so do these others take all the individuality out of plainchant.

It is, then, upon the art of plainchant interpretation that I wish to concentrate, without falling into the temptation, often well-nigh irresistible (and indeed already succumbed to!), to wander down bypaths of history, aesthetics, or technics. I have endeavoured to make the following pages severely practical, saying little, except incidentally, or for a special purpose, of matters concerning the history of the chant, the structure and rhythm of the melodies, the mechanics of singing the chant, the pronunciation of Latin, and so forth, that have received ample treatment elsewhere, as the bibliography will show.

It will be clear, therefore, that the practical use of this book presupposes a choirmaster familiar with the language of plainchant, and certainly one who is no obscurantist, no liturgical crank, but a musician, an explorer, a man of common sense.

In defining my position in the ' political sphere ' of the chant, I make gladly and sincerely the usual genuflections in the direction of Solesmes. But I can accept only as many of their conclusions as march with my

* *Work and Leisure*, p. 101. Eric Gill. (Faber.)

artistic convictions: basing myself upon first-hand contact with text and music, with due, but not slavish, deference to tradition, to the findings of the *Motu Proprio*, to the Preface of the Vatican Gradual, and to a careful examination of the only system other than that of Solesmes which deserves consideration.

That the comparative accuracy of the Vatican text is due to a monk of Solesmes is a matter for which we should indeed be grateful to the Benedictine order, true in this to their great traditions of scholarship, and one may safely say that it represents the original text as nearly as may be*.

Most of us will wish to possess as well as the Vatican edition the well printed and labour-saving books with the rhythmic signs of Solesmes, those of Grenoble, and any other reputable versions that may be produced; just as, though the parallel is not exact, in our study of Bach's ' 48 ' we do not confine ourselves to the original text, but consult the editions of Tovey, Busoni, Brooke, etc.

Reasonable liberty must be allowed to the choirmaster, for no vital interpretation ever came from the mere observance of rules and regulations. I am quite ready to have the ideas put forward in this book debated, but I shall be much surprised if they can be held to conflict in any way with the *Motu Proprio* or with any rulings of Our Holy Mother the Church, to whom I protest my complete loyalty and obedience.

It cannot be sufficiently strongly stated that though most of plainchant may be essentially monastic the parish church is not a monastery, the choir is not composed of monks, there is a congregation, not of a plainchant intelligentsia, but of ordinary men and women who should be allowed some means for the release of their emotions (through the Ordinary of the Mass and the Responses)—abundantly offered them in the Anglican Church—and some vital appeal to their inherent sense of beauty (through the Proper of the Mass).

I dread the uniformity of treatment, the regimentation to which, in deference to mistaken ideas of Solesmes' teaching, plainchant is often subjected, and which causes people to find the Church's official music so wearisome to listen to and priests reluctant to have time spent on its performance. What chance with such handicaps has the lyrical beauty, the dramatic force, of this offertory or that antiphon, of reaching the hearts of men and reinforcing the teaching of the Liturgy!

We return to the starting-point of these discursive reflections. There must be a lively apprehension of the senses before there is any appreciation of the mind. The great religious music of Bach, the tremendous issues which Beethoven confronts, Elgar's deeply felt music to *The Dream of Gerontius*, have power to move the hearts of men, these composers being unafraid to use all the resources of the musical art.

---

* See, however, ' The Vatican Edition of Plainchant,' by H. Bewerunge, *Irish Ecclesiastical Record* (Jan. 1906), which contains some important criticisms.

And I believe that the Gregorian composers or compilers—they were something of both—did the same within the limits of their chosen medium. They strove to find a real tonal embodiment of the words and thought in order to add greater efficacy to the text and move men to greater devotion. We wish, indeed, to meet with peace and holiness in our churches, but always with reality, spiritual and artistic. The monastery of its nature withdraws from the world, the parish church enters it to try and touch and hallow men's lives at all points. The chant must therefore be interpreted to conform to these conditions.

It must frankly be said, also, that no good is done to plainchant by the frequent denigration of modern music made by certain Solesmes writers. Dom Gajard compares the poverty-stricken system of our two modes, major and minor, with the rich variety of the plainsong modal system; but the handling of those two wretched modes by a line of great composers from Bach to Brahms has produced results not entirely negligible. Nor should it naïvely be assumed that all modern music is written for the titillation of the nerves, or that it is a continual tearing of passion to tatters!

Dom Gajard claims that the supple melodic line of plainchant can express ' *les sentiments les plus opposés, avec toute la gamme de leurs nuances: la joie, la crainte, la douleur, l'espérance, la supplication, la prière, l'amour surtout, mais l'amour divin, car elle ne connaît que celui-là: l'inspiration religieuse, qui la dirige toujours, l'empêche de s'égarer. Aussi sa liberté ne dégénère jamais la mesure; tout est ordonné, calme, serein, tranquille, jusque dans l'enthousiasme et la douleur. Caput artis decere, disaient les anciens: elle garde toujours les supremes convenances*.'*

I entirely agree with the writer that the range of emotion in plainchant is very great, but I regret his apparent wish to have the chant put into the charge of a Censor of Emotions!

Can grief, fear, joy, hope, all be expressed calmly, serenely, tranquilly? Or, rather, should they be so expressed? The Church has left the catacombs now and can lift up her voice! The Alleluia chant heard first in the fourth century was the cry of the victory of Christianity after two and a half centuries of persecution. It is all very well to tell us that ' *la matière sonore n'existe plus par elle-même; elle est tout entière au service de l'esprit, informée et vivifiée par lui. . . .*' And later, that ' *Cet art ne cherche jamais l'effet; il ne se complait pas en lui-même, il bannit tout ce qui est virtuosité, il n'existe que pour Dieu*†'.

The first point I have abundantly dealt with, but to say that virtuosity is banished in the chant is to ignore the facts of history and turn a blind eye and a deaf ear to a great many graduals and tracts which require, indeed, to be sung with virtuosity or not at all. There is no reason to suppose that Almighty God dislikes virtuosity so long as it is used for His honour and glory and not that of the singer!

* *La Musicalité du Chant Grégorien*, p. 25. Dom Gajard. (Desclée, 1931.)
† *Ibid.*, p. 37.

What records are there of the way in which plainchant was actually
sung in the average parish church of the Middle Ages? I imagine that
there are very few. But we can still see the realism of the frescoes of
the people's picture gallery—the walls and arches of the church—we
can read in their library—the service books and the doctrinal sermons—
and wonder if the moment the choir or the people began to sing they
fell into the lady-like, namby-pamby, pernickety imitations of French
monastic chanting—a thing beautiful in itself, in its proper setting—
that are often heard to-day.

I do not for one moment believe it. Let us then feel and express the
lyrical beauty of an *Ave verum corpus*, the drama of a *Tenebrae factae
sunt*, without unnecessary inhibitions but in obedience always to the
true artistic instinct of what is fitting and proper; what is due to the text
and music, its purpose, and the place where it is performed.

Now in spite of the repeated orders of Councils and Bishops that the
chant should be suitably rendered in parish churches, that priests
must carefully learn the chant for the whole year round, and have
a clerk competent to sing, we may reasonably conclude that the common
people, at least, found the chant nearly as remote and abstruse as they
find it to-day in spite of the distant likeness it bore to their own song.
Nor would the people have been the more reconciled to the Church's
official music by reason of her unwavering, though not always successful,
opposition to their self-made music and to the minstrels who moved
amongst them. Nevertheless, there must have been many pieces with
an affinity to their own music, such as some of the settings of the hymn
Iste Confessor, that they loved to sing in and out of church, others such
as the *Dies Irae*, literary and musical counterpart of the Doom painting
that usually hung above the arch leading to the Sanctuary, that deeply
stirred them; and the very fact that the idiom of the Proper of the Mass
may have appeared remote to them, and so affects people to-day, is
a tribute to its specifically religious and other-worldly character.

To expect plainchant to be popular is as unreasonable as to expect
chamber music to be popular: but a more encouraging lead from the
clergy and the musicians in the organ loft might end in a great deal of
the chant finding appreciation in quarters where its beauties go unsus-
pected or are obscured by finicking and unworthy performance.
I conclude this preliminary survey of a difficult subject with an apt
quotation from ' Catholicism as Unconscious Art ', a stimulating essay
by Terence White that appeared in the January 1935 number of
Blackfriars.

' Art and Catholicism have been in conflict, but ideally they should
form a perfect unity. For the conscious existence of anything ever seeks
to blend itself with the unconscious, and the unconscious to lose itself
in consciousness: the body and the mind are the conscious and fallible
expression of the soul, and, as St Augustine has said, " all the life of the
body is the soul ". Thus all the life of art is Catholicism: Catholicism

may be called the super-ego of art. But equally Catholicism has a duty to recognize art. Two errors must be avoided, that spirit disowns matter, and that spirit automatically includes matter: the errors respectively of Manichaeism and Spinozism. But art is more than the body or even the mind of Catholicism: it has true rights of its own. (Just as art must recognise ritual, and ritual obey dogma, so must dogma obey that spirit or principle of art by which the whole of Catholicism is a poem, and which alone compels the obedience of ritual to dogma, and the recognition of ritual by art.) '

CHAPTER II

TECHNICAL POINTS

1. NOTATION

The first section of this chapter and most of the second section have been written for those who are unfamiliar with the square notation of plainchant and the rhythm peculiar to the chant, and merely give sufficient information to enable the examples in this book to be read and sung with ease. Fuller treatment, historical and practical, of these subjects will be found in manuals such as *The Grammar of Plainsong*. The section on rhythm is also intended as a modest clarification of the two main ideas on this much-debated subject, which so often generates more heat than light.

Both sections are, of course, mainly compilations taken from the various sources noted in the bibliography at the end of this book.

Stave. The four-line stave is used, with occasionally an extra small line above or below it to accommodate a larger range of notes than it allows.

Clefs. Two clefs will be found on this stave, the C clef (any line of the four upon which C, or *do*, is placed) and the F clef (the line upon which F, or *fa*, is placed). A small 'guide' placed at the end of each stave gives the pitch of the note on the next stave.

C Clef   F Clef

Accidentals. The one permitted accidental, B flat, remains in force until the natural (♮), or a bar line, or a new word, cancels it.

In the Grenoble and some other versions the square notation is placed upon a five-line stave with the G clef and a 'key signature'.

O   vós   óm - nes,*

In the traditional notation this example would appear as below.

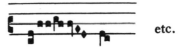

etc.

The reading of the chant is considerably simplified thereby, but the
' key signature ' is apt to give a wrong impression of the modes.

A number (or numeral) above each piece denotes in which of the eight
modes it is written, and the addition of a letter, e.g. 8F, in the case
of the antiphons, the ending that is to be given to the appointed psalm
tone. The reader must go to one of the plainchant manuals for information on the modes and kindred subjects outside the scope of this book.

MARKS OF DIVISION.
(See the section on phrasing, p. 23.)

SINGLE NOTES.

(1) *punctum* (square note).
(2) *punctum* (diamond note).
(3) *virga* (tailed note).
(4) *quilisma*.

It is the look of the notes rather than their strange names that the
reader should commit to memory. (Nos. 2, 3, and 4 will only be found
in combination with other notes.) These single notes are *all* represented in modern notation by the quaver, for though they differ in
shape, they all have the same approximate time value.

| Punctum | Virga | Diamond |

NEUMS OR GROUPS

TWO-NOTE GROUPS.
(5) *bistropha* (see *strophicus*, No. 18).

Bistropha

(6) *podatus*=an *ascending* group of two notes, the first or lower of which has a musical accent (i.e., a slight stress) while the second is usually lighter.

Bistropha Podatus

(7) *clivis*=a *descending* group, the first or higher note carrying a musical accent.

Clivis

THREE-NOTE GROUPS.
  (8) *tristropha* (see No. 18).

Tristropha

(9) *scandicus*=an *ascending* group of three notes with the musical accent on the first note.

Scandicus

(10) *salicus*=a group very similar in shape to the *scandicus* but (in most editions) having the first note slightly detached from its fellows. The musical accent falls on the *second* note.

Salicus

(11) *climacus*=a *descending* group of three notes with the musical accent on the first. The diamond-shaped notes are not shorter, nor are the tailed notes longer than the square characters. All the notes are of equal time value.

Climacus

(12) *torculus*=a group of three notes with the musical accent on the first. It must be sung as three equal notes, and bears no relation to the triplet of modern music.

Torculus

(13) *porrectus*=a group of three notes in which the second descends from the first. It owes its odd shape to the labour-saving use which the scribe made of his pen. This accounts also for the diamond notes of the *climacus*.

Porrectus

(14) The *podatus* (6), *clivis* (7), *scandicus* (9), and *torculus* (12) are all found in liquescent forms as below. The little note is used at the meeting of two consonants (or two vowels forming a diphthong), e.g. *palma—ad te—magnus*, etc. Some authorities hold that the liquescent

note should be sung lightly, others that it should be fully produced and even slightly lengthened. This is a matter of individual taste.

Epiphonus (podatus) *Semivocal Torculus* *Cephalicus (clivis)* *Liquescent Scandicus*

(15) *quilisma*=an expressive device consisting of a kind of turn. The first note immediately preceding the *quilisma* in the group in which it occurs, which has the musical accent, is not doubled but lengthened to about half again of its value of one beat. The *quilisma* note itself must be given its proper value of one beat, and is not shorter than the one which follows it. It is usually sung lightly.

Quilisma

(16) Groups are formed from all the above of four, five, or more notes, but these should offer no difficulty to the reader who has memorised the first groups. The initial note of each neumatic group carries always (with the two exceptions given) 'a delicate renewal of rhythmic energy* '; an expression I owe to Father A. G. Macdonald's polemical but excellent pamphlet *Plainsong for the People* (Universe office).

(17) It remains to describe the *pressus*, which is the juxtaposition (at the same pitch and on the same syllable) of two *neums* or of a *punctum* and a *neum*.

Pressus

In the second example the musical accent is drawn from the first note of the second *neum* to the last note of the first *neum*, the two notes forming the *pressus* being sung strongly or softly according to the nature of the text.

(18) The *strophicus*, or repetition of one or more notes at the same

* The reader should consult the text-books in regard to the position of secondary accents in neums of more than three notes.

pitch, is quite distinct from the *pressus*, as it requires, theoretically, a separate ' tongueing ' of each note.

Strophicus

As it would require a highly skilled choir to avoid giving an impression of bleating in carrying out this effect, it is usually wiser to have the notes held for the requisite number of beats while swelling out the tone towards the last note.

It is to be hoped that the strange-sounding names of the notes and note-groups will not have intimidated the reader.

It is true, and not a mere antiquarian fancy, that the square notation gives a far more faithful picture of the melodies than a whole string of quavers, the effect of which is to dazzle the eye and render analysis difficult.

To aid further the reader completely unskilled in this notation I have added a ' key-signature ' (giving the note on the clef line which is Do*, and a beginning note above every example as far as Chapter VI), but the ' key-signature ' must be thought of as indicating only pitch, not tonality, and as conveying no idea of the mode. This ' key-signature ' and starting note will appear always thus: (G : g), etc.

The purpose of the asterisk in the musical examples is to mark off the intonations at the start and to indicate where the choir join in again with the Cantors, or divided portion of the choir when these have been singing alone, as in, for example, the *Gloria Patri* of the *Introit* or in the versicle of the *Alleluia*.

2. PLAINCHANT RHYTHM

A great many of the supposed complexities of plainchant rhythm vanish in the act of singing, but a clear understanding of this rhythm is fundamental to a vital interpretation of the chant.

None of the systems advanced are to be regarded as dogmas to subscribe to the whole of which is necessary for the salvation of the musical soul, and only two now require any serious consideration at all, the Solesmes system, and the system loosely known by its opponents as accentualist. Briefly speaking, Solesmes declares that not only the rhythm conditioned by the text must be taken into account, but also the rhythm inherent in the music; the ' accentualists ' base themselves almost entirely upon the rhythmic influence of the text upon the music.

With the exaggerations of either of these schools, more to be found in their followers than in their promoters, I do not propose to deal, since the purpose of this section is only to state basic principles and to recon-

* The sharps or flats implied by the key of this note are to be understood.

cile differences perhaps more apparent than real; but I have alluded in a section below to the evil of hammering the accents, the ponderous and exaggerated *tenuto* of which Dom Gregory Murray speaks*, which is a constant danger of 'accentualism', and to the peril of excessive rhythmic analysis into which the disciples of Solesmes are apt to fall.

In considering the nature of plainchant rhythm it is important to remember that, as Dom Gatard says, the chant ' has its own rhythm, and that well marked and not essentially different from that of modern music '.

Here we can use Dom Mocqueareau's excellent definition of rhythm: ' Rhythm is the passage from movement to repose '; and the sense of rhythm can be awakened in the mind not only by (1) a succession of sounds varying in intensity or dynamic force, but also by a succession of sounds varying in (2) length or (3) pitch. This passage from movement to repose, a continuous rise and fall (to a point of cadence), with certain notes given prominence in the various ways stated in the previous section for the establishment of rhythmic order, becomes subject to the fact that all music (as all language) divides itself up into binary and ternary groups, and is so comprehended by the mind. I give the language examples in English in order to make this doubly clear†.

Binary. One ' strong ' syllable and one weak.

PRÁISE THE / LÓRD HIS / GLÓRIES / SHÓW

Ternary. One ' strong ' syllable and two weak.

PRÁISE TO THE / LÓRD THE AL/MÍGHTY, THE / KÍNG OF CRE/ÁTION.

Now plainchant, like prose, knows of no regularly recurring and divisible beat as does measured music, for the beat in the chant, represented by the quaver-unit, is indivisible, though it may be lengthened; and the binary and ternary groups are mixed at will, producing the free rhythm which alone can make long stretches of unaccompanied melody acceptable to the ear. With accents occurring at absolutely regular intervals, as in measured music, plainchant would become as square as its notation and intolerable to listen to. The following examples of free prose and its musical equivalent show how the binary and ternary groups may be mixed.

THÓU ART THE / KÍNG OF / GLÓ - RY O / CHRIST:

THÓU ART THE / É - VER / LÁSTING / SÓN OF THE / FÁTHER.

---

* *Gregorian Rhythm*, by Dom Gregory Murray, p. 30. (Catholic Records Press.)
† I am indebted to Francis Burgess's *Rudiments of Plainchant* (*Musical Opinion* office) for the examples below.

The reader should now have a mental picture of the plainchant notation sorting itself out into binary and ternary groups, and these into composite groups, half-phrases and phrases*, an arsis (rise) which in the long sweep of a phrase may well comprise a number of falls, and a thesis (fall) which may comprise a number of rises; the melody ever rising with a gentle *crescendo* and falling with a similar *decrescendo*, with a *delicate renewal of rhythmic energy on the first note of every distinct neum, binary or ternary, unless that neum happens to be a pressus or a salicus,* in which case, as we have seen, the accent is displaced.

I have spoken so far of musical accent, but we need not assume warfare between this and the verbal accent of the text to which the music is allied. In syllabic chant (one syllable=one note) all agree that the music receives its rhythm from the words so that if the text is binary or ternary, or if it be mixed, the music will follow suit. The note lengths are indeterminate in that they vary according to the time required to enunciate the syllables.

Such a rendering may well be called modulated reading, and is best seen and felt in the ancient liturgical recitatives. Here is a portion of the Ferial *Pater Noster*.

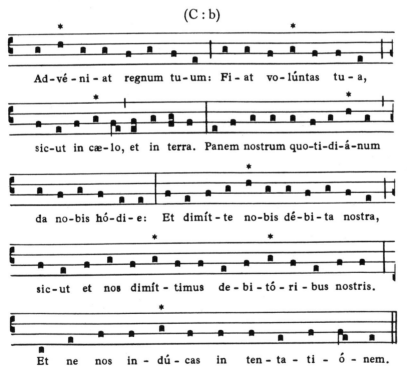

---

* The Solesmes analysis of the chant into feet, bars, phrases, sections, and, finally, the period, is unnecessarily confusing.

In the treatment of the ornate or melismatic pieces, the 'accentualist school' declare that the music still derives its rhythm from the Latin text, the rhythm being oratorical, so that in fairly ornate chants the tonic syllables of the words will form the principal accents, but that in entirely ornate chants the accents of the culminating neums (and that of the *pressus*) will always have a relative importance when the force of the verbal tonic accent has spent itself; and that in neums of more than three notes one must distinguish always between principal and secondary accents, but that even the weakest syllable of a word will serve to support one or more neums.

But if it is true that the 'accentualist' school wish to hold that the principal or tonic accent of the Latin text is *necessarily* a strong accent, a strong down beat—and this is how it is frequently made to sound— then one can only say that the evidence of the treatment of this accent by the Gregorian composers proves the reverse often to be the case, for, as will be seen below—and it is the same in example after example— the tonic verbal accent is given to one note only, and the non-accented syllable receives a neumatic group of notes.

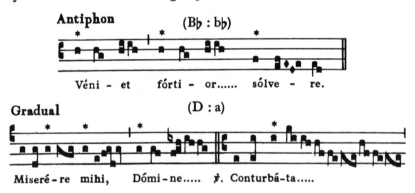

From these examples—to which there are naturally exceptions—it is not difficult to deduce that the Gregorianists favoured an essentially light, short 'up-beat' Latin tonic accent* and to follow with the fact that the down-beat (the fall or cadence on which will then occur the weak syllable) is not necessarily (or often) strong.

Dom Gregory Murray has given some interesting examples of the practice of the polyphonic writers in this respect which reveal them holding to the same idea of a light, short tonic accent and a down-beat not necessarily strong†; and Dr Schweitzer, in his great book on Bach, gives many instances of the 'up-take' character of Bach's phrasing which it may be interesting to quote here.

Speaking in general terms, says Schweitzer, ' the axiom is that in Bach the accented note is not the commencement but the end of the group '.

---

* But nothing approaching *staccato*.

† *Gregorian Rhythm*, by Dom Gregory Murray, pp. 21-22. (Catholic Records Press.)

The grouping that is usual elsewhere (a) is the exception with him: the grouping that is unusual elsewhere is with him the rule (b).

In the first *Kyrie* of the B minor Mass, ' Bach throws strong counter-accents on to the second and fourth beats and, by means of the antagonism between this and the natural bar accent, ensures the animated variety of rhythm necessary for the elasticity of his figures '*.

That the down-beat is not of its nature strong in modern music (still less in the chant) may be seen in the correct phrasing of the well-known G minor organ fugue and in the Franck example.

Fugue in G minor. Bach.

Fugue in B minor. Franck.

Even if the organ were capable of percussive accent its use would be unnecessary as the accents in Bach's passage from movement to repose are beautifully marked merely by the melodic elevations, and it is the up-beat and not the down-beat that stands out.

Rhythm is established by cadences where rest is taken before the next flight, and these points of cadence are the so-called *ictus* or footfalls of the rhythm, in essence neither strong nor weak, but, as cadences, pertaining to length rather than to strength.

Of the rhythmic signs to be found in the Solesmes books it is, then, principally the *ictus*, the rhythmic carrier-beat, which represents a bone of contention. Solesmes tell us that stress will only be connected with it if change of pitch and duration are lacking; but if the verbal tonic accent—which, after all, is and must remain the chief accent in all circumstances, however we mix our dynamic shades of intensity, or however the accent be expressed by shortness, length, or melodic elevation—coincides with the *ictus* (or down-beat cadence) the latter becomes reinforced.

The rules for placing the ictus, so far as they affect the first or second notes of the *neums*, according to the nature of the *neum*, need worry no one, as they run according to the generally accepted laws of plainchant rhythm, and if at other points Solesmes' teaching upon the

* *J. S. Bach*, by Albert Schweitzer (translated by Ernest Newman), Vol. II, p. 381. (Black.)

question of the *ictus*, which I do not wish to discuss further here, fails to convince the reader, he must study the alternative system of Dom Lucien David*.

There is no doubt that singers who follow the Solesmes system are apt to become over-anxious about this largely mental *ictus*, and fussed and distracted by the type of cheironomy thought necessary to insure its observance. The result is, very often, timid and emasculate singing.

Simplification in exposition is needed, and less of the careful but too exhaustive rhythmic analyses to which choirs are sometimes subjected. Let them visualize and sing whole phrases and not worry so much about minute divisions and sub-divisions.

It would be unfair to Dom David, whose *Méthode Pratique* is the best statement available of the true ' accentualist ' position, not to say that there is much that is valuable in his book, especially as regards interpretation—though he, too, falls a victim to the peculiarly French passion for minute analysis and takes six pages to explain the singing of the first sentence of the *Agnus Dei*!—and that it is laudably free from the slight symptoms of persecution mania that disfigure some of the writings of Solesmes. All who have some French should read it, for Dom David's position is often not justly put by his opponents.

The Vatican text itself has no rhythmic signs and the Preface is curiously silent on the question of plainchant rhythm, but it clearly presupposes that the singing shall move with a true *legato*, not a level tone in which all the notes will have the same validity, so inducing a fatal monotony, but a *legato* in which verbal accents, principal and secondary, and the footfalls of the rhythm have their rightful prominence. Moreover, in the drawing of the smooth melodic line there will be the tonal shading caused by the gentle *crescendo* to a climax and the *decrescendo* from it, so typical of the chant; and other characteristics such as the softening of the last note or notes in varying degree at the end of the rhythmic divisions marked by the so-called bars and the *rallentandos* at the ends of the pieces. True musical phrasing will be an integration of all these things and of every other aspect of the music hereafter mentioned. These things taken into account, the chant will ' sing itself '!

At the same time most choirs will certainly need a text with some rhythmic signs, and I have chosen the Solesmes text for the musical illustrations as being, on the whole, the most practical. (Dom David uses a single rhythmic sign in his Grenoble books, a sign of prolongation.)

Two words of warning. We may adopt the Solesmes rhythmic signs, wholly or partly, but we should not feel bound to adopt the French style of singing. ' *Angli jubilant, Alemanni ululant, Itali caprisant, Galli cantunt*,' wrote a French monk long ago. And we may still jubilate and leave the French to sing (as they like to call it), the Germans to howl, and the Italians to caper if they feel like it. But let us not scruple to

* See Bibliography, p. 111.

adopt the Italian method of pronouncing Latin (see the manuals), for it is by far the most musical.

Finally, let us remember that ' were we even to attempt by a particularly accurate notation, and by multiplied signs, an execution which we could believe would be mathematically exact, the same difficulties (of rhythm) would still subsist, for we cannot represent by material signs that which will be always immaterial and indefinable*'.

The warning is needed. 'Half-a-dozen experienced organists were asked to play the thirty-two stolid minims of a hymn-tune, and no two of them played them alike in point of time. All prolonged an accented and most a high note, and all slowed down at the end; but all did all these things in varying degrees.' If this was the case in measured music, how much more so in free rhythm, and we may be thankful for this ' fringe of unstrictness ' and that the extra something which escapes all rules cannot be enchained in words and become standardized.

THE SOLESMES RHYTHMIC SIGNS

A punctum may be affected in four ways:

1. ♪   2. ♪   3. ♪   4. ♪ •

1.   The vertical episema (ǀ) denotes a rhythmic ictus.

2.   The horizontal episema (–) denotes *slight* prolongation of the note to which it is added.

3.   The double episema (ī) denotes a rhythmic ictus and *slight* prolongation.

4.   A dot added to a note indicates that such note is to be doubled.

Groups of several notes may be affected by the episema or the dot, as follows:

The choirmaster will naturally come to an agreement with his choir as to the observance, or, on occasion, non-observance, of these rhythmic signs, and familiarize them with the method of conducting he adopts.

For the sake of comparison I have set out the Vatican text, together with the Solesmes and Grenoble versions, of the hymn *Pange Lingua*. In the Solesmes version the vertical *episemas* show where the *ictus* falls, and the dotted notes mark the ' exact ' length of the *rallentandi*. For the latter purpose Grenoble uses a slur.

---

* *Plainsong*, by Rev. T. Helmore, p. 18. (Novello.)   c

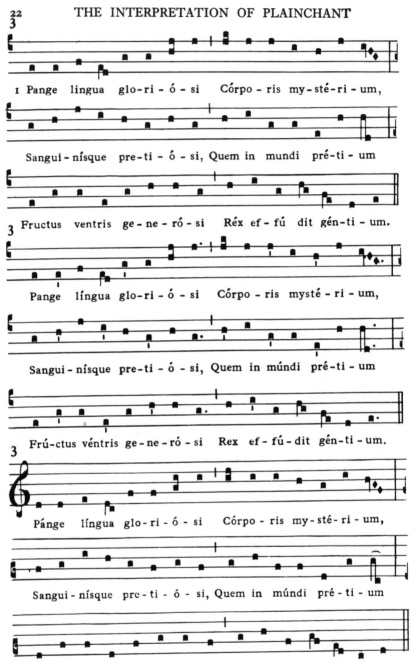

1 Pange lingua glo-ri - ó - si Córpo - ris my-sté-ri - um,

Sangui - nísque pre-ti - ó - si, Quem in mundi pré-ti - um

3 Fructus ventris ge - ne - ró - si Réx ef - fú dit gén-ti - um.

Pange língua glo-ri - ó - si Córpo - ris mysté - ri - um,

Sangui - nísque pre-ti - ó - si, Quem in múndi pré-ti - um

3 Frú-ctus véntris ge - ne - ró - si Rex ef - fú-dit gén-ti - um.

Pánge língua glo-ri - ó - si Córpo - ris my-sté-ri - um,

Sangui - nísque pre-ti - ó - si, Quem in múndi pré-ti - um

Frúctus véntris ge - ne - ró - si Réx ef - fú - dit gén-ti - um.

All other marks of expression, slurs, etc., made in the musical examples are added by me.

3. PHRASING

The use of so-called ' bars ' in modern editions of the chant, vertical lines which mark the end of rhythmical divisions and have no relation to the bars of modern music, make phrasing a matter of no great difficulty so far as the mechanics of it go. These bar lines have, of course, the effect of punctuation, and their literary equivalents are, roughly, as follows: ¼ bar = , — ½ bar = ; or : — whole bar = ; or . — double bar = . At these bars there can be (1) a slowing down of the previous notes, (2) a breathing place, (3) a pause.

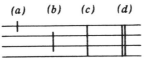

It is generally agreed that there will be no *rallentando* and no respiration (unless it is absolutely necessary), and no pause at the quarter-bar: no *rallentando*, a breathing place, but no pause at the half-bar; very little *rallentando*, a breathing place longer than at the half-bar, and a pause at the whole bar. At the double-bar, which marks the end of a piece, a considerable *rallentando*. This is the strict letter of the law, but individual practice will differ as to how it is or is not applied. The length of the pause or of the *rallentando* cannot, of course, be precisely laid down: it will depend on taste and on the *tempo* adopted for the piece*.

It may be added again that though a slight or a greater softening of the note or notes preceding these bar-lines will have the effect of indicating the logical divisions of the music, the long phrases that are one of the joys of plainchant (and of all music) must not sound as if chopped into little sections. On all counts the quarter-bar is the danger: for in plainchant as in modern music the very presence of a vertical line suggests a traffic signal at danger to the singer, and he stops! These small divisions must not be made excuses for breathing unless, as, for instance, before the melismatic phrase at the end of the versicle of an *Alleluia*, or before any lengthy neumatic group, a new breath is really required. One often hears the *Te lucis*, or other hymns, sung with a pause at the quarter-bar instead of being felt and sung in two complete phrases without a pause at the quarter-bars.

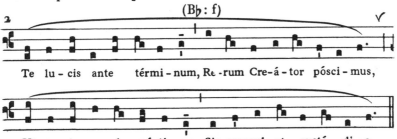

Te lu - cis ante térmi - num, Re -rum Cre-á - tor pósci - mus,

Ut pro tu - a cle - ménti - a, Sis praesul et custó - di - a.

* Any tendency to drag must be at once checked: most choirs sing the chant too slowly.

Before the ending of the day,
Creator of the world, we pray
That with thy wonted favour thou
Wouldst be our Guard and Keeper now.

There are, at the same time, many instances, as in the examples below, where a small but perceptible break should be made at the quarter-bar, as when certain words or half-phrases need to be isolated for special emphasis or clarity, or if there is a strong feeling of cadence on the notes preceding the quarter-bar. But such examples as that of *Lutum fecit* need careful treatment so as not to sound affected or scrappy.

(D : a)

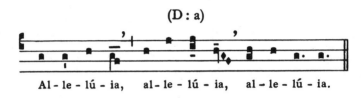

Al - le - lú - ia, al - le - lú - ia, al - le - lú - ia.

(C : b)

ut vi - gi - lémus cum Chrísto, et requi - es - cá - mus in pa - ce.

(That we may watch with Christ and rest in Him.)

4 (D : g)

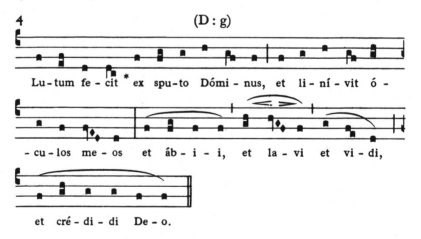

Lu - tum fe - cit * ex spu - to Dómi - nus, et li - ní - vit ó -

- cu - los me - os et áb - i - i, et la - vi et vi - di,

et cré - di - di De - o.

(The Lord made clay of spittle, and anointed my eyes: and I went, and I washed, and I saw, and I have believed in God.)
No quarter-bars divide the three *Sanctus* in the following Antiphon,

but, as in the *Te Deum*, or in the *Kyriale* settings, a fraction of a pause
should be made between each repetition.

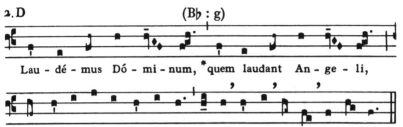

Lau - dé - mus Dó - mi - num, *quem laudant An - ge - li,

quem Ché-ru-bim et Sé - raphim Sanctus, Sanctus, Sanctus proclámant.

As has been said, the *rallentando* before the whole bar will be of a
length dictated by the movement of the whole piece, and also by the
sense of the text. The Antiphon *Mitte manum tuam* (p. 36) is an instance
where, as the previous notes have received a *rallentando*, another is felt
to be out of place and the final *Alleluia* is sung in the time of the whole.

The above statements, then, are certainly not to be taken as binding
universally.

These points observed, phrasing as an artistic whole is only just begun.
Dom Gregory Murray has well observed: ' Our first approach to
Gregorian melody must be through a thorough understanding of its
text, which must be followed by an examination of the particular interpretation of the text chosen by the composer. The general lines of our
interpretation are settled by the words; the particular expression of each
musical phrase is settled by the rise and fall of the melody; the careful
grading of the phrases suggested by the relative importance of their
respective climaxes leads to an artistic rendering which is not only faithful
to the meaning of the words but also to the requirements of the music*'.

In other words, the phrasing of the chant follows upon the lines of all
musical phrasing and is, above all, the result of a feeling for the melodic
line in its integrity. The plainchant singer should experience some of
the sensations of the tight-rope walker on his flexible steel wire. A little
too much weight this way or that and he is over: so in the chant too much
emphasis here or there and the flexible melodic line is pulled out of shape.

I assert again that the singer who can deal with such things as Schubert's
Nacht und Träume, Brahms's *Feldeinsamkeit*, or Wolf's *Schlafendes
Jesu Kind*, will have little difficulty with the phrasing of the chant.
A study of the two great arts of plainchant and *lieder* singing side by
side will benefit both.

Long-breathed phrases sung in such a way that one feels the singer
has reserves of breath, can draw back here or hasten a little there, is in
full command of melody and word, is distributing his accents, verbal
and musical, so as to give due place to each, is preserving the continuous
smooth flow of the chant along the valleys and up the hills of its points

* *Music and Liturgy*, p. 73. January 1936.

of climax throughout a whole rhythmic period, such an art of phrasing
will alone bring out the true beauties of the chant.

4. THE LATIN TONIC ACCENT AND ACCENT-HAMMERING

One of the greatest evils that can befall the chant is the hammering
of the Latin accents, primary and secondary, the result of which is to
destroy the true *legato* which should characterize the singing of the
chant in particular and, indeed, all good speaking or singing.

The look of a hammered-out text in print should suffice to show how
great is the distortion to the ear in the equivalent of sound.

glÓRia pÁtri et fÍLio

This easy way of singing the chant, jumping from ' strong ' accent to
' strong ' accent and letting what comes in between take care of itself,
becomes intolerably wearisome to the ear and is subversive of any
sensitive interpretation.

The essential lightness of the Latin tonic accent cannot be insisted
upon enough—it is testified to by example after example in this book—
and this accent is very frequently put into sufficient relief by its melodic
elevation, so that little, if any, further emphasis is required.

In the ancient liturgical recitatives and syllabic chants the natural
emphasis the speaking voice would give to the principal verbal accents
is beautifully secured simply by melodic elevation. And in neumatic
and ornate chants, also, the same means are frequently taken to throw
the tonic accent into relief. No better examples could be given than the
ones below, which show five different settings of the same words*.

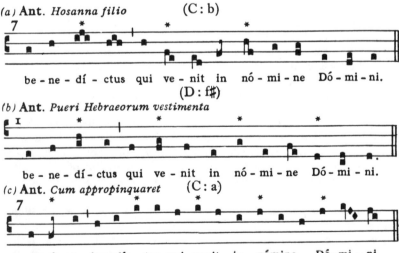

(a) **Ant.** *Hosanna filio*   (C : b)

be - ne - dí - ctus qui ve - nit in   nó - mi - ne   Dó - mi - ni.
(D : f♯)

(b) **Ant.** *Pueri Hebraeorum vestimenta*

be - ne - dí - ctus qui ve - nit in   nó - mi - ne   Dó - mi - ni.

(c) **Ant.** *Cum appropinquaret*   (C : a)

Hosánna,   benedíc - tus qui venit in   nómine   Dó - mi - ni.

* *Estetica Gregoriana*, by Abbot Ferretti, pp. 20-1. (Pontifical Institute of Sacred
Music, Rome.)

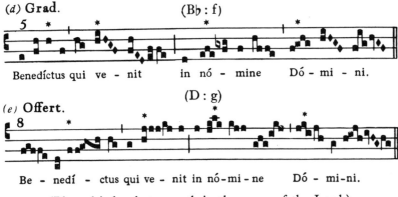

(*d*) **Grad.** (B♭ : f)

Benedíctus qui ve - nit in nó - mine Dó - mi - ni.

(*e*) **Offert.** (D : g)

Be - nedí - ctus qui ve - nit in nó-mi-ne Dó - mi-ni.

(Blessed is he that cometh in the name of the Lord.)

It has been well said that the nature of the Latin tonic accent is much better brought out by the approach to it (*crescendo*), and the departure from it (*diminuendo*) than by a piston-like precision on the accent itself, which is melodic rather than intensive. It is of its nature on the *up-beat*, since for the Latins the last syllable of the words was the resting-place or down-beat, while the life of the words was the tonic accent. Hence the saying: '*Accentus anima vocis*'.

If we sing (in the *Magnificat* Antiphon, Common of One Martyr, 1st Vespers):

fun-dát-us é-nim é - rat _____

—and uninstructed singers will be drawn to the 'strong' accents as a needle to a magnet—the true nature of the accent is brutalized and the phrase thrown out of proportion. Follow this up by letting melodic elevation alone mark the accent:

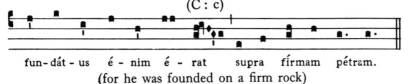

(C : c)

fun-dát - us é - nim é - rat supra fírmam pétram.
(for he was founded on a firm rock)

and immediately the chant acquires that immateriality and flexibility which is one of its great charms.

Allied to accent-hammering, and so fitly to be mentioned here, is the practice of hitting at the final (weak) accent of a word and swelling out the tone on it. This is as irritating in the saying as in the chanting of the Liturgy, and it violates the constant rise and fall implicit in the very construction of the Latin words.

Sing *Kyrie eleison*, as is so often done, with a *crescendo* on the final weak syllable:

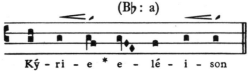

and then with the right accentuation, and the difference will at once be perceived.

It is, indeed, a good thing to keep a picture of the verbal triangle formed by the Latin word in the mind, for the construction of the Gregorian melodic line follows the same law of construction, and the Gregorian musical period—adding melodic to verbal line—says Abbot Ferretti, whose examples I quote below, is formed like an arch.

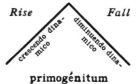

This ' arch ' may be seen in the antiphon below rising from *videntes* to the point of climax (*domum*) and falling to its other base (*myrrham*).

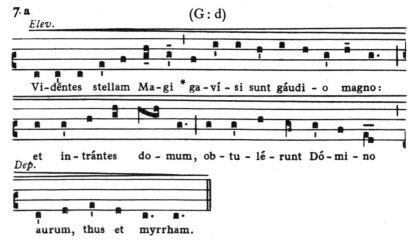

(The wise men seeing the star rejoiced with a great joy: and entering the house brought to the Lord gold, frankincense, and myrhh.)

5. The Asterisk

Care should be taken not to produce a burst of tone at the asterisk, particularly if it cuts into the literary or musical sense of a phrase. The ' join ' should be effected with a minimum amount of disturbance unless, of course, the text indicates an increase of tone, as at the first repetition of an *Alleluia*.

6. Psalms and Antiphons

The treatment of the psalms must be entirely and completely objective, whether or no the psalm rejoices or mourns. A *De profundis* or a *Jubilate* will be sung at precisely the same speed and with the same degree of tone.

The reason for this is that ' the verse which serves as the antiphon text contains the fundamental thought of the psalm to which it is sung, and indicates the point of view from which it is to be understood. In other words, it gives the key to the liturgical and mystical meaning of the psalm, with regard to the feast on which it occurs* '. So, then, the antiphon is to receive subjective, expressive treatment, and it is the antiphon alone that will break the gentle communal rhythmic current of

crescendo and *decrescendo* ⟨ ≥ * ⟩ set up by the psalm

tones and carried on by each side of the choir. If we were to start differentiating between psalm and psalm, why should we not do so when some notable change of sentiment takes place within the psalm or canticle?

In the *Magnificat* is ' *deposuit potentes de sede* ', to be sung loudly, and ' *et exultavit humiles* ' softly, is the first part of Psalm 59 (*Deus repulisti nos*), to be sung slowly because it cries out that God has cast off his people, and then quickly and loudly at the sixth verse, when the psalm begins to rejoice! And is Psalm 28 (*Afferte Domino*) to be rendered as a Rossinian storm-piece?

How, moreover, is such differentiation really to be secured?

To take an example at random. The third psalm of the Second *Feria* at Vespers begins ' *Ad Dominum cum tribularer clamavi : et exaudivit me* ', the cry of a soul in trouble. The fourth psalm expresses hope: ' *Levavi oculos meos ad montes : unde venient auxilium mihi* '; and the fifth joy: ' *Laetatus sum in his quae dictae sunt mihi : in domum Domini ibimus* '. Now these three emotions are beautifully indicated in the antiphons which precede and follow each psalm. In these antiphons such emotions can find expression and be meditated upon while the even current of the psalm continues. It is not that we do not think of and clearly enunciate the words in the psalm, but that, though the heart may speak powerfully, thought takes the lead and tells us that a continuous unvarying current of chanting is the only practical, and aesthetically right, way of singing the psalms communally.

* *Catholic Encyclopedia*. Art. ' Antiphon '.

Any tendency to swell out the tone or to prolong the notes at the cadence points should be checked, and the length of the pause at the mediant (the asterisk) should be of the value of a crotchet relative to the *tempo* adopted. No pause need be made at the end of each verse, as the verse will be sufficiently distinguished from its fellows by the difference in timbre between the two sides of the choir, or between choir and congregation. A pause at this point destroys the flowing rhythmic current that is one of the beauties of psalmody. As brisk a *tempo* as is compatible with the clear enunciation of the words on the reciting note (the dominant) should be adopted.

The Sunday psalms for Vespers and Compline are available in the second volume of *Plainsong for Schools*, though, unfortunately, without a version in the vernacular, and one can only hope that congregations can be induced to give their allegiance once again to these beautiful Offices in place of the ' popular ' type of service which has replaced them. One has heard boys' schools sing the psalms of Sunday Vespers with heartening enthusiasm—if with a sublime disregard for nuance!— and there is no real reason why any average congregation should not do the same, given a little clear encouraging instruction free from unnecessary technicalities.

7. Hymns and Sequences

Plainchant most nearly approached the music of the people in its iambic and trochaic hymns. Many of them, Cecil Gray says, are ' definitely metrical and syllabic in contrast to the ordinary Gregorian chant and sometimes have a distinctly pagan allure '; and St Ambrose is said to have fascinated the people with the melodic charm of his hymns.

We do not want to emphasize the pagan allure, and interior evidence shows that the Gregorian composers tried to get away from the metrical scheme of the words in their music, but their treatment of these hymns leaves us with many tunes that only require to be known and experienced to become popular. Such tunes are those to *Te lucis* (setting for Sunday), *Ave Maris Stella* (1), some of the settings of *Iste Confessor* (2, 5, 8), *Jesu Redemptor Omnium, Creator alme siderum, Deus tuorum militum* (1), etc. Miss Glyn, in her most interesting book on the ' Evolution of Music ', quotes a reference in which priests are spoken of as ' praising God with psalms and hymns, giving time to the oarsmen ' during a mercifully smooth Channel crossing. Now oarsmen must row rhythmically and in regular periods and we need not fear, while avoiding metrical squareness, to sing these hymns with an attractive rhythmic swing.

The sort of thing that is to be avoided is singing the most popular setting of *Iste Confessor* (No. 2) so squarely that it is virtually put into the shackles of common time.

Ist - e con - fessor Domin-i col-en - tes

It may be worth remarking here how considerably the Solesmes rhythmic signs can change the musical rhythm of a hymn. In the Vesperal (Vatican edition) the hymn *Omnis expertam* appears without, of course, any dotted notes:

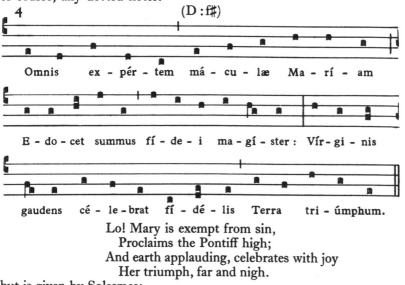

Lo! Mary is exempt from sin,
Proclaims the Pontiff high;
And earth applauding, celebrates with joy
Her triumph, far and nigh.

but is given by Solesmes:

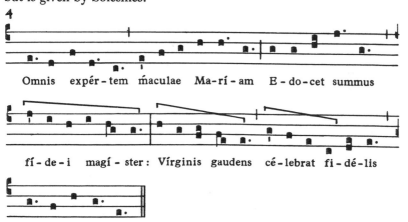

Ter-ra tri-úmphum.

We are free to choose either version. (Notice the sequences I have marked in the Solesmes version.)

The four beautiful Sequences* that are left to us in the Roman Liturgy are all miniature music dramas. These sequences, ' rhymed and

* I follow Abbot Ferretti in speaking of four rather than five Sequences, since the *Stabat Mater* is rather a trochaic hymn than a Sequence.

rhythmical sequence in verses grouped in strophes, almost in the manner of hymns ', may fitly be considered here. Only four remain in the Roman Missal out of the many attributed to Notker (+912), and it is much to be hoped that some of the others, said to be of great beauty, may be restored to use.

These four Sequences—*Victimae Paschali* (Easter), *Veni, Sancte Spiritus* (Pentecost), *Lauda Sion* (Feast of *Corpus Domini*) and *Dies Irae* (Mass for the Dead)—are all well known. Their melodic construction is conditioned by the beautifully free form of the poems, and the first, *Victimae Paschali*, is an especially lovely little liturgical drama.

With the exception of the first and eighth verses (or strophes) the verses run in pairs, new melodic ideas clothing verses 2, 4-5 (treated as one unit, and, of course, repeated at 6-7) and 8 (a phrase from 2 but a new conclusion). The *Amen-Alleluia* is a later addition.

Verses 1-3 should be sung by the whole choir; verse 4 either by one or more male voices; verses 5-7 by a treble soloist, and the conclusion by all*.

(D : e)

Vic - ti - mæ paschá - li láu-des *ímmo - lent Christi - á - ni,

Agnus re - dé - mit ó - ves: Chrístus ín - no-cens Pá - tri

recon - ci - li - á - vit pecca - tóres. Mors et ví - ta du - él - lo

confli - xé - re mi - rándo: dux ví - tæ mórtu - us, régnat vívus.

Dic nóbis Ma-rí - a, quid vi-dís-ti in ví - a? Sepúlcrum Chrísti

vivén-tis et, glóri-am ví-di resurgéntis: Angé - licos téstes,

* I owe this suggestion to Abbot Ferretti. *Canto Gregoriano*, p. 135. (Desclée.)

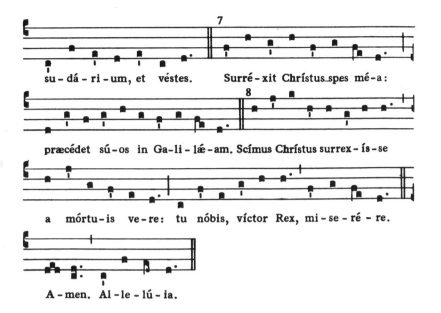

su - dá - ri - um, et véstes.   Surré - xit Chrístus_spes mé-a:

præcédet sú-os in Ga-li - læ-am. Scímus Chrístus surrex- ís-se

a mórtu- is ve - re: tu nóbis, víctor Rex, mi - se - ré - re.

A - men. Al - le - lú - ia.

Prelude

1ᵃ Victimae pascháli láudes
immolent Christiáni,

2ᵃ Agnus redémit óves:
Chrístus ínnocens, Pátri
reconciliávit
peccatóres.

3ᵃ Mors et víta duéllo
conflixére mirándo:
dux vítae mórtuus,
régnat vívus.

4ᵃ Dic nóbis María,
quid vidísti in vía?

5ᵃ Sepúlcrum Chrísti vivéntis
et, glóriam vídi
resurgéntis:

6ᵃ Angélicos téstes,
sudárium, et vestes.

7ᵃ Surréxit Chrístus spes méa:
praecédet súos in
Galilaéam.

Conclusion

8ᵃ Scímus Chrístum surrexísse
a mórtuis vere:
tu nóbis, Victor Rex,
miserére.

(Christians, your sacrifice of praise
To the Paschal Victim raise.

The Lamb has all the sheep redeemed:
Sinners Christ, the undefiled,
Has to His Father reconciled.
Life with Death, and Death with Life,
Strove, and their vast duel seemed
Strange and unexpected strife:
Life's Captain, who on that day died,
Lives and reigns now, glorified.

Tell us, Mary, tell us, pray
What saw you upon your way?

I saw the tomb where Christ had lain,
And saw Him, living once again,
In His risen glory dight;
And the Angel witnesses;
Yea, and e'en the napkin white
And His grave-clothes met my sight.
Christ, my hope, arisen is;
And before you He will go
Into Galilee.
                 We know,
As the truth itself has said,
That Christ has risen from the dead.

O Thou, who wonnest victory thus,
Our King, Thy mercy show to us.*)

8. The Approach to the High Note at a Point of Climax

A good Solesmes rule is to approach a high note of climax with a
crescendo that culminates in a *piano*. This must not, of course, be done
in the sudden dramatic way that Wolf employs†—in this case on
a repeated note—but rather as it is felt in the long-rising phrases of
Brahms's *Feldeinsamkeit.*

er schuf die Schönheit und dein An - ge - sich

---

* Quoted from *Hymns from the Liturgy*, by Rev. J. Fitzpatrick, by kind permission
of Messrs Burns & Oates.
† *Gesegnet sei. Italienisches Liederbuch.* Hugo Wolf.

Von Himmels blau-e   wunder-samen wo-ben,Von Himmels blau-e

wun-der-sa-men   wo - - ben.

It is interesting to note that Beethoven often follows a *crescendo* with a *piano*. The variations in the first movement of the A flat pianoforte Sonata (Op. 26) offer a well-known example of this marking.

This rule will have exceptions suggested by the nature of the text. Thus, if we compare the two Graduals, *Flores** and *Omnes de Saba* (p. 46), which use some of the same material for the Versicle, we shall probably feel that the sweeping *illuminare* phrase in the second Gradual should be brighter toned, louder, than in the first Gradual, where the delicacy and tenderness of the text suggest a soft, floating tone at *Veni*.

Once again, all such points must be settled not by the nature of the music but of the text, to which the music must ever be subservient.

9. CHANGES OF SPEED

The usual places for the employment of a *rallentando* are mentioned in the section on phrasing, but, as we have seen in that section, there are often occasions where the text demands special emphasis—a slower *tempo*, a pause, an *accelerando*, and so forth. These devices should be unhesitatingly used to give greater point and intelligibility to the music, but always in a disciplined and artistic manner.

Here are some instances (other than those pointed out elsewhere in the course of the book) where a slower *tempo* than in the rest of the piece may well be adopted.

8   (B♭ : b♭)

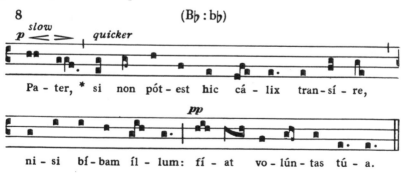

Pa - ter, * si   non pót - est hic cá - lix tran-sí - re,

ni - si bí-bam íl - lum: fí - at   vo - lún - tas tú - a.

('Father, if this Chalice may not pass by, except I drink of It : Thy Will be done.')

* Feast of the Apparition of B.M.V. Immaculate, Feb. 11.

The value of the notes strictly observed almost carries a sufficient *rallentando*, but a degree more is necessary. Very soft tone.

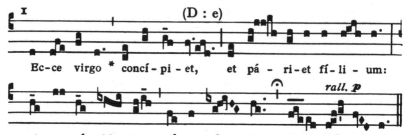

Ec-ce virgo * concí - pi - et, et pá - ri-et fí - li - um:
et vo - cá - bi - tur nómen é - jus Em - má - nu - el.

(Behold, a Virgin shall conceive, and shall bear a Son : and His Name shall be called Emmanuel.)

Here a slight pause before *Emmanuel*: the whole phrase should be sung softly and slowly with a small *crescendo* to a *piano* on the vowel ' a '.

8. G *

Spí - ri - tus * qui a Pa - tre pro - cé - dit, al - le - lú - ia:
il - le me cia-ri - fi - cá - bit, al - le - lú - ia, al - le - lú - ia.

(The Spirit Which proceeds from the Father, alleluia : It shall enlighten me, alleluia, alleluia.)

If the Solesmes signs are observed in this example they constitute, in fact, *tempo rubato*, which should be paid back by *no greater a degree of rallentando* on the last *Alleluia* than is implied in the dotted notes.

8. G *   (D : g)

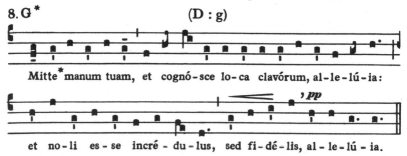

Mitte * manum tuam, et cognó-sce lo-ca clavórum, al-le-lú-ia:
et no - li es - se incré - du - lus, sed fi - dé - lis, al - le - lú - ia.

(Put forth thy hand, and know the marks of the nails, alleluia : and be not unbelieving, but faithful, alleluia.)

To bring out the full significance of *fidelis* as opposed to *incredulus*, sing it slowly with a decided soft emphasis, and pick up the time in the *Alleluia*, to be sung very softly.

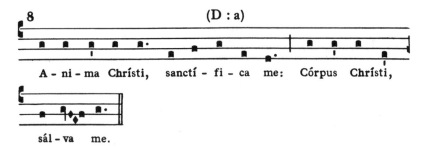

A - ni - ma Chrísti, sanctí - fi - ca me: Córpus Chrísti,

sál - va   me.

(Soul of Christ, sanctify me : Body of Christ, save me. Blood of Christ, inspire me.)

This motet can be made one of the loveliest things in plainchant, but it will depend on ignoring the rhythm-destroying dot in the middle of each first phrase (Solesmes version), and in beautiful *rubato* handling of the Schubertian turn at the end of each verse. Alternate verses may be taken by solo voices.

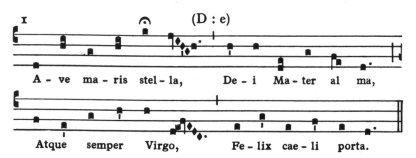

A - ve ma - ris stel - la,   De - i Ma - ter al   ma,

Atque   semper   Virgo,   Fe - lix cae - li   porta.

(Hail, Star of the Sea, gracious Mother of God and ever a Virgin, blessed Gate of Heaven.)

I heard a choirmaster insert this pause one day when the men were ' off ' and he had only his trebles. The bright star-point of tone, with the subsequent run down, proved effective and not in the least bit cheap. It was a daring idea, a deliberate distortion, if you like, but justified in performance: though it should not be done in the remaining verses. (The hymn was, of course, being sung as a motet.)

The same melody is used for both the following antiphons, but whereas in the first antiphon (for the Common of Doctors) a *ritardando* is natural at the name of the Doctor commemorated, in the second antiphon (one of the great ' O's ' that fall in the third week of Advent) a slight *ritar-*

D

dando not at the same point of the melody, but at *Veni*, is imposed by the word on the music. In the one case the cadence is a mere footfall of the melody, in the other a more definite resting point.

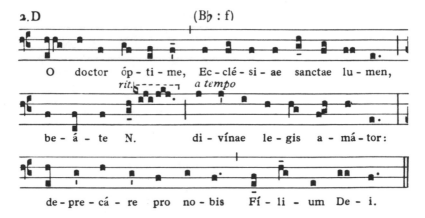

(O excellent Teacher, thou light of the holy Church, blessed N., lover of the divine law, entreat for us the Son of God.)

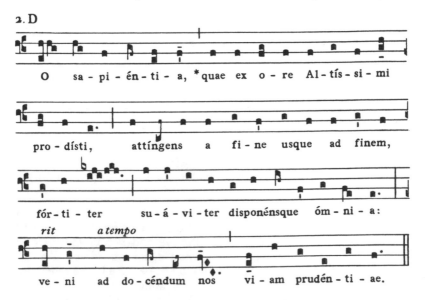

(O Wisdom! that proceedest from the mouth of the Most High, reaching from end to end mightily, and sweetly disposing all things: come and teach us the way of prudence.)

10. THE MELODIC ECHO

An immediate repetition of the *jubilus* phrase is sometimes found in the *Alleluias* and their Versicles, and also in other places. Such an obvious source of tonal contrast should not be, as it often is, disregarded.

In the *Alleluias* the repetition is either exact or, in fact, a melodic imitation which develops to a point of climax, or two separate phrases may be repeated. In the first example below, and all such, a beautiful effect is secured if the repetition is sung softly, indeed as an echo of the preceding phrase. But in the second example given a continuous *crescendo* to the high point of climax—a *crescendo* embracing the characteristic rise and fall of the plainchant phrase—is called for.

The power of development possessed by the Gregorian composer is well seen in the construction of this Alleluia.

I give the third *Alleluia* in full, that is with its versicle, so as to show the need for carefully thinking out the tonal contrasts to be used. Too many echo effects would be cheap and out of place, and a long *crescendo* is preferable at the *jubilus* of the versicle.

pá - ti Chrí-stum, et re-súge-re a mór -
- tu-is, et i - ta in-trá - re in gló -
- ri - am * sú - am.

Alleluia

(℣. It behoved Christ to suffer and to rise again from the dead, and so to enter into His glory. Alleluia.)

In the Offertory *Sperent in te* there is a good example of the same kind of echo-phrase treatment (twofold) (p. 98), and there are innumerable instances of small melodic figures being repeated in this way.

For the sake of comparison I give some instances from modern music—the keyboard and vocal music of the sixteenth, seventeenth and eighteenth centuries contains many—which may be interesting. Similar examples may, of course, be found in the music of all periods.

Single phrase-repetition:

Samson. Handel.

Tot - al e - clipse   no sun!   no moon!

Orpheus. Gluck.

No true artist would sing the repeated phrase with exactly the same degree of tone as at ' *No sun* '; and in the same way contrast of tone is called for in the Gluck example. As an instance of threefold repetition, marked *diminuendo*, I have taken a phrase from one of the pieces in the

FitzWilliam Virginal Book. The literature of the two-manual harpsichord, no less than that of the organ, abounds in such passages.

The Fall of the Leafe. Martin Peerson.

11. COUNSELS AND WARNINGS

' Let each strive to sink his voice lowly into the consort of the choral song. Let us abhor every affectation of voice, all ostentation and singularity, and whatever calls up the histrionick; nor let us copy those who fling forth the chant too lightly, or those who utter the syllables with undue pomposity: let us rather sing every chant with such solemnity, yet with such movement that we sing alway with ease of voice and a full sweet tone.'—(Hucbald (840?-930), Nicetas, Instituta Patrum.)

' The Fourth Council of Carthage prescribed the following words to be spoken at the so-called ordination (by a presbyter, not a bishop) of the Canons, or singing men, in the newly formed Schools of Chant (fourth century): " See that thou believe in thy heart what thou singest with thy mouth, and approve in thy works what thou believest in thy heart."

' And first it is requisite that the words which are being sung shall be clearly and rightly understood.'—(Benedict XV, 1854-1922.)

' It is a matter of necessity that the singer shall command respect for his skill as well as for his voice, so that not only by the merit of the words, but also by the sweetness of the music, he may raise the souls of his hearers to the remembrance and love of heavenly things.'—(Council of Aix-la-Chapelle, 816.)

' On these grounds Gregorian Chant has always been regarded as the supreme model for sacred music, so that the following rule may be laid down: The more closely a composition in Church Music approaches in its movement, inspiration and spirit the Gregorian form, the more sacred and liturgical it becomes; and the more it is out of harmony with that supreme model, the less worthy is it of the Church.

' The ancient traditional Gregorian Chant must therefore be largely restored in public worship, and it must be held for certain that an ecclesiastical function loses none of its solemnity when accompanied by only this kind of music.

' Special efforts are to be made to restore the use of Gregorian Chant among the people, so that the faithful may once more take an active part in the Church offices as was the case in ancient times.'—(*Motu Proprio* (1903). Pius X.)

Traditional Views on the Singing of the Chant

Speaking of performances of the chant after the foundation of the *Scholae Cantorum* (fourth century), Mr Henderson says*:

' In a mass of details, some of which are confusing and others contradictory, one conclusion shapes itself clearly, namely, that the chants were not sung in a dull and monotonous manner. The trained singers filled them with richness and variety.'

Among the vocal ornaments used he notes the two following: *Trill*, known perhaps in the first century, certainly in the third. Pomponius Festus, the grammarian, defines it thus: '*Vibrissare est vocem in cantando crispare* '.

Portamento. First written record by Guido of Arezzo (first half of eleventh century). ' The voices melt together in many after the manner of the letters, so that one tone begun seems limpidly flowing into another and not to be completed.' The author then alludes to marks of expression and of time, ' known at least as far back as the closing years of the 8th century ', in a paragraph which I summarise below.

' The Romanian letters in the antiphonary of Romanus of the Abbey of St Gall† (ninth century) included:

C (*celeriter*)= *accelerando* (*leggiero ?*)
T (*tenere*)= hold
M (*mediocriter*)= *moderato*

and letters denoting degrees of force or modification (e.g., *bene* modifying T=*molto ritardando*).'

St Bernard (1090-1153), in his regulations for the singing of the chant at the Abbey of Citeaux, writes: ' It is necessary that men sing in a virile manner and not with voices shrill and artificial like the voices of women, or in a manner lascivious and nimble like actors '.

The Scotch Abbot Aeldred, writing in the twelfth century, speaks of the singers whinnying like horses, using gestures, swaying their bodies, twisting their lips, rolling their eyes, and even bending their fingers with each note.

' These singers, infatuated with themselves and with the sacred order by which they were called, loved to cultivate their long hair, of which the luxuriance, displayed on their soft silken dalmatics—as the beautiful semi-Byzantine mosaics of SS Cosmas and Damien (at Rome) show us— added without doubt, as they thought, to the effect produced by their voices, when in view of all the people they delivered from the ambon the verses of the sacred melody.'—(*L'Art Grégorien*, p. 16. A. Gastoué. Alcan.)

* *Early History of Singing*, pp. 24-5. W. J. Henderson. (Longmans, New York.)

† Series II, Tome II, *Codex* 359 *de la Bibliothèque de Saint-Gall* (*Paléographie Musicale de Solesmes*) is still in print, and costs £2 10s.

' Synging and saying of Mass, Matins, or Evensong, is but roryng, howling, whistelyng, mummying, conjuryng and jozelyng and the playing at the organys a foolish vanitie.'—(' Seventy-Eight Faults and Abuses of Religion ' presented to Henry VIII in 1536.)

' The tedious plainsong grates my tender ears.' (*Lingua*, before 1607.)

' What tears I shed at Thy hymns and canticles, how acutely was my soul stirr'd by the voices and sweet music of Thy Church. As those voices enter'd my ears, truth distill'd in my heart, and thence divine affection well'd up in a flood, in tears o'er flowing, and happy was I in those tears.'—(St Augustine, *Confessions*, ix, 6.)

' Yet when it happens to me to be more moved by the music than by the words that are sung I confess that I have sinned (*poenaliter peccare*), and it is then that I would rather not hear the singer.'—(*Ibid.*, x, 33.)

' What would St Augustine have said could he have heard Mozart's Requiem, or been present at some Roman Catholic Cathedral where an eighteenth-century mass was perform'd, a woman hired from the Opera-House whooping the Benedictus from the Western Gallery.'— (Bridges, *Collected Essays*, xxii. Oxford University Press.)

' And if we consider and ask ourselves what sort of music we should wish to hear on entering a church, we should surely, in describing our ideal, say first of all that it must be something different from what is heard elsewhere; that it should be a sacred music, devoted to its purpose, a music whose peace should still passion, whose dignity should strengthen our faith, whose unquestioned beauty should find a home in our hearts, to cheer us in life and death; a music worthy of the fair temples in which we meet and of the holy words of our Liturgy; a music whose expression of the mystery of things unseen never allow'd any trifling motive to ruffle the sanctity of its reserve. What power for good such a music would have.'—(*Ibid.*)

' The great principle, the fundamental canon, the rule of rules for the right execution of the *neums* is LEGATO; that is to say that " the sounds in one group of notes, in practical execution, must be bound together as closely as possible*." '

' The first condition, indispensable and necessary to ensure the Gregorian melody becoming lovely and expressive, is *good, correct, and accurate declamation joined to a flowing delicate smooth execution of the neumatic groups*†.' (Italics mine.)

* *Canto Gregoriano.* D. Paolo M. Ferretti, Abbate, O.S.B., p. 66 (Desclée).
† *Ibid.*, p. 105.

CHAPTER III

TYPICAL LINES OF STUDY

Plainchant will have nothing to say to the choirmaster who opens his Gradual or Vesperal only at the choir practice, regarding the minimum that must be sung as a dreary dribble of notes to be dispatched as quickly as possible. But he who takes the trouble to discover the unity of thought which so beautifully informs the Mass and flows into its musical setting, meditating upon all the contributory factors of diction, rhythm, tone, speed, pitch, etc., that fuse into a just interpretation, will have spent his time well and be well rewarded.

There is a type of plainchant purist who will insist upon having everything sung without any reference to the abilities of his choir, the time at his disposal for rehearsal, the possible tediousness of a Gradual or a Tract (for not all plainchant is equally inspired!), or the need to introduce the welcome relief of polyphony*. This is both foolish and irreverent.

The proper balance must be decided by the choirmaster, and, indeed, nothing must be left to the spur of the moment.

I have worked out two lines of study which cover at least the essential points and may serve as a useful guide, but must only be considered suggestive. (How much controversy we should have been spared if only the medieval theorists of the song schools had done something like this instead of leaving us treatises which, if interesting and useful as regards tonality and rhythm, leave us practically in the dark as to interpretation.) Once again let me plead for the greatest possible variety of treatment consistent with the medium used. Every page of this book insists that the words are the starting-point and inspiration of the music. Even in the case of the adapted melodies this will be interpretatively true. The text and music, therefore, must be *thought* as a whole by the choirmaster.

SCHEME FOR THE FEAST OF THE EPIPHANY OF OUR LORD:
Doctrinal

Without being a theologian, the choirmaster will be able to remind his choir (in case they are not all those ' men of known piety and probity of life ' envisaged by the *Motu Proprio*!) of the significance of the Feast, and this is the first point upon which he should inform himself.

Dom Lefebure's *Daily Missal* (or Dom Cabrol's) gives more than sufficient matter for this purpose.

' Epiphany ' means ' manifestation ', and on this day God reveals His Son (Collect). ' Christmas ', says Fr. Martindale in another book the choirmaster will find useful, *The Mind of the Missal*, ' is a tender and human feast '. 'But not one of its Masses permits us to forget that the

* The book of *Abridged Chants* (Desclée), consisting of Graduals, Alleluias and Tracts set to ancient psalmodic formulas, will often be found useful.

child whose birth we commemorate is God. Our eyes see Bethlehem; but our faith must read into Eternity; and adoration must always be at the heart of our rejoicings.'

There are then two special ' notes ', one exterior and one interior, to be brought out, the appealing picture of the visit of the Three Kings and their tender adoration of the infant Jesus with which our own worship is mingled.

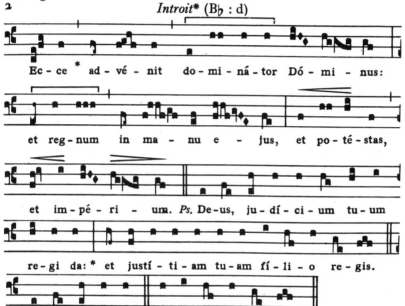

*Introit** (B♭ : d)

Ec - ce * ad - vé - nit do - mi - ná - tor Dó - mi - nus: et reg - num in ma - nu e - jus, et po - té - stas, et im - pé - ri - um. *Ps.* De - us, ju - dí - ci - um tu - um re - gi da: * et justí - ti - am tu - am fí - li - o re - gis.

Gló - ri - a Patri. E u o u a e.

(Behold *the Lord the Ruler is come*: and the Kingdom is in His hand, and power, and dominion. Ps. lxxi. 2. Give to the king Thy judgment, O God: and to the king's son Thy justice. ℣. Glory be to the Father.)

' Behold the Lord the Ruler is come.' The kings are travelling to the King of kings. This approach may be brought out by the treatment of the confident interval of a fourth at '*dominator*' and '*et regnum*', which should be sung with a slight emphasis and increase of tone, reaching a climax at ' *potestas et imperium* '. Do not soften much at the close. The psalm (as I have said in the section of psalmody in the chapter on Technical Points) must be sung softly and quite objectively.

Kyrie† (C : g)

No. II (*Fons bonitatis*) from the Ordinary is a good choice if a polyphonic setting is not used.

* I have used the plain Vatican text for all the musical illustrations in this chapter, wishing to avoid confusion between my own and Solesmes' markings.
† I say nothing about the Ordinary of the Mass, which belongs by right to the congregation, for the singing of this raises problems that lie outside the scope of this book.

Gloria (F : a)

Gradual
(If possible in C:f, but if too high, in B)

(All they from Saba shall come bringing gold and frankincense and showing forth praise to the Lord. Arise and shine, Jerusalem: because the glory of the Lord has arisen upon thee.)

There is some gorgeous verbal imagery to be illustrated vocally in the succeeding pieces of the Proper.

The caravan sets forth in the swinging phrases of ' *omnes* '—' *Saba* '—' *annuntiantes*,' and the shapes of the climatic *neum*-groups, all related to one another, should be felt in these three phrases.

The Versicle *Surge* (boys' voices only) should be sung more quickly and vigorously than the preceding section, and then follows the great sweeping phrase at ' *illuminare* ', with the top note like a spearpoint of shining light (which certainly does not mean that it is to be shouted), approached with a *crescendo* and a gradual *accelerando* as marked. The phrase at ' *Domini* ' will be sung softer, as if the full significance of the rising of the glory of the Lord had dawned upon the singers.

The conventional fifth tone end is disappointing after the magnificence of the rest of the music.

Alleluia (B : F♯)

Slower

Al - le - lú - ia.   * *ij.*   ℣. Ví - - di - mus   stellam   e - - jus   in   O - ri - én - - te,   et   vé - ni - mus   cum muné - - - ri - bus   ad - o - rá - re * Dó - mi - num.

(℣. We have seen His star in the East, and *are come with gifts to adore the Lord*. Alleluia.)

The key phrase is the tender ' *adorare Dominum* ' of the versicle, which may well be gradually approached from ' *vidimus* ' or, at least, ' *venimus* ', with a subtle, slow but continuous softening of tone, and a decided *rallentando* at ' *adorare* ' up to the end, with a very clean attack after the asterisk.

Credo No. 3 (E♭ : b♭)

Offertory (B♭ : b♭)

5

Re - ges Tharsis   * et ín - su - læ mú -

- ne - ra óf - fe - rent: re - ges A - ra - bum

et Sa - ba   do - na ad - dú - cent:

et ad - o - rá - bunt e - um   omnes re -

- ges ter - ræ, o - mnes gen - tes sér - vi -

- ent   e - i

(The kings of Tharsis and the islands shall offer presents: the kings of
the Arabians and of Saba shall bring gifts: and *all kings of the earth shall
adore Him: all nations shall serve Him.*)

In the same tone as the Gradual but happily without the conventional
ending. The phrases lengthen out from the bare statement of ' *reges
Tharsis* ' to the romantic ones of ' *Arabum et Saba* '—the last with a
characteristic ' echo '. The downward scale passage at ' *insulae* ', and the
more extended ' *adducent* ' to be sung very smoothly as if making a picture
of the kings bowed down in adoration. ' *Adorabunt* ' is, of course, the
' leading motive ' of the whole piece. Not only these kings, but all the
kings and people of the earth, adore and serve Him. ' *Omnes* ' (a three-
note *neum* twice repeated—*gent(es)*—*serv(ient)*—must be sung broadly,
then decrease the tone at each repetition to a soft close.

Sanctus (D : d) *and Agnus Dei* (D : e)
(There is no reason why, sometimes, the final *Hosanna in Excelsis* should not be sung quite softly. In any case it must not be shouted.)

4   *Communion* (C : e)

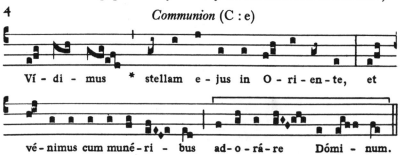

(We have seen His star in the East, and *are come with gifts to adore the Lord.*)

The oriental atmosphere is preserved in the opening phrase, which is of much the same pattern as that used at the opening of Rimsky Korsakoff's *Scheherazade!* (See also the versicle and response at Vespers.) Notice the accentuation of ' *ejus* '—the Gregorianists care for the Latin tonic accent. Here again the key phrase is the tender ' *adorare Dominum* '. (Compare this Communion with the versicle of the Alleluia above.)

The Epiphany Mass offers a fine field for pictorial illustration, but in order to remove any impression that this is all one looks for in interpreting the chant, I have chosen for the next Mass that of the twenty-third Sunday after Pentecost, in which such illustration is reduced to a minimum. It has been said that the music of the chant often interprets the text in a way that far transcends our ordinary thoughts, and that is why, for example, the '*Resurrexi* ' of Easter Sunday is so different from the joyful upspringing sort of melodic figures we should expect. The treatment of the text is the musician's individual conception of its religious significance, his tonal meditation upon its content: and in this way one composer may be literal and another mystical.

SCHEME FOR THE MASS OF THE TWENTY-THIRD SUNDAY AFTER PENTECOST
Doctrinal

' The season after Pentecost is the symbol of the long pilgrimage of the Church towards heaven; that is why the last Sundays describe to us prophetically its last stages*.' There is an undercurrent of anxiety fluctuating through the Mass in spite of God's assurance, in the Introit, that he thinks thoughts of peace and not of punishment, and the encouragement of the Communion telling us that whatever we ask in prayer, believing that we shall receive, that shall be done to us. This anxiety may be further brought out by choosing a low pitch for the various pieces of the Proper.

* *Daily Missal*, p. 1162. Dom Lefebure. (Coldwell.)

6

Introit (D : e)

(The Lord saith: I think thoughts of peace, and not of affliction: you shall call upon Me, and I will hear you; and I will bring back your captivity from all places. Ps. lxxxiv, 2. Lord, Thou hast blessed Thy land: Thou hast turned away the captivity of Jacob. ℣. Glory be to the Father.)

Adopt a deliberate pace and sing *Dicit Dominus* softly. The asterisk coincides with the opening pronouncement so that the increase of tone comes happily at ' I think thoughts of peace. . . .' The intonation formula is repeated at ' *cogita*(*tiones*) '. It may here be noted that though a right instinct prompts us to give the words of Our Lord, spoken in the first person, to a solo voice, because He was possessed of a human as well as a divine nature, the words spoken by God should always be sung by the choir. God the Father was never depicted in early mosaics and wall paintings, but always God the Son.

The contrast between peace and punishment is well expressed by the introduction of the B flat in the familiar formula set to (*afflict*)*ionis*. Sing the three notes of the accented syllable of ' *invocá*(*bitis*) ' with a slight swelling out of tone. The whole phrase from ' *et reducam* ' to the double bar should be sung, if possible, in one breath.

Kyrie (XI, *Orbis Factor*) (C : a)

Gloria (B♭ : g)

Gradual (G : e)

(Thou hast delivered us, O Lord, from them that afflict us: and hast put them to shame that hate us. ℣ In God we will glory all the day: and in Thy name we will give praise for ever.)

Consider Gradual and Alleluia as being complementary. The emotion of praise at deliverance from enemies grows through the Gradual and overflows into the *Alleluia*, but is checked by remembrance of sin.

The pace adopted should be quicker than that for the Introit. Sing '*confundisti*' robustly with a slight emphasis on the *torculus* group ('dí'), but no softening of tone: and then with the smallest possible break at the quarter-bar resume the original *tempo*, and at the close neither make a considerable *rallentando* nor greatly soften. A solo voice (tenor) is the most effective for the versicle, and should give full effect to the lovely phrase '*laudabimur tota die*', the climatic point of the whole versicle. Sing the 'echo' phrase at '*in saecula*' with fuller tone than at '*confitebimur*', and feel how the concluding phrase grows out of it.

7   *Alleluia* (G : d)

(℣. From the depths I have cried to Thee, O Lord: Lord, hear my prayer.—Alleluia.)

Quicken the pace again a little at the *Alleluia**. The piece is a good example of a theme stated, repeated and developed. It should be sung with the exuberance of tone an *alleluia* usually requires, but, when

* Alleluias, like all plainchant, are nearly always sung too slowly and ponderously.

the theme appears again at the end of the versicle, the whole of which should be taken at a slower pace, the emotional significance of ' *de profundis* ' must darken the tone. The fluctuating emotions of the Mass will be brought out at the *reprise* of the *Alleluia* when the same theme will be given its original tempo and exuberance of tone. The phrase at ' *exaudi* ' requires the passage from *crescendo* to *piano*, of which I have spoken in ' Technical Hints '.

Credo I or III
Sanctus (B♮ : g)
Offertory (B♮ : d)

(From the depths I have cried out to Thee, O Lord; Lord, hear my prayer: from the depths I have cried out to Thee, O Lord.)

The structure of this beautiful piece is ternary: A-B-A. The Cantors must give the opening syllabic notes out distinctly and unhurriedly, and the choir make the form clear by a considerable *rallentando* at ' *Domine* ' and at ' *meam* ' and a complete break. The music covers exactly an octave, and again at ' *exaudi* ' comes the highest note, though it does not have the principal accent on this occasion. The phrase ' *Domine exaudi vocem meam* '—one breath up to ' *meam* ' then a quick, deep intake of breath for the melismatic phrase, following with its graphic descent to the low d—should be sung by a soloist. This will give full effect to the repetition of *de profundis*, etc.

E

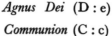

(Amen I say to you, whatsoever you ask when you pray, believe that you shall receive, and it shall be done to you.)

The cadences are shaped in the same way as those in the Introit, though modally distinct, but perhaps it is worth remarking on this liaison between the words of God in the Introit and those of Our Lord in the Communion. Give the music a soft tone of quiet confidence and check any tendency to hurry or slur over the syllabic notes.

CHAPTER IV

THE GREGORIAN COMPOSER AT WORK

THE ANTIPHON 1F

In a *Sunday Times* article on Sibelius, Ernest Newman says: ' Sibelius, like every other composer, unconsciously casts his ideas into a dozen or so type-formulae and type-procedures that recur, in whatever veiled forms, in everything he writes '.

The Gregorian composers did the same thing, but consciously. Original melodies abound, but over and over again the chant (text and music) is a patchwork or mosaic (*melodie-centoni*) of formulas, as the great Benedictine musicologist, Abbot Ferretti, has convincingly shown in the first volume of his *Estetica Gregoriana*. He gives a table of five formulas of intonation and twelve central formulas, and applies these to thirty-two verses of text with a figure over each phrase giving the formula used. Then, with formidable industry, he tabulates another thirty-seven formulas and applies them similarly to forty-four lines of text.

' Now the *Painters' Guide* found by M. Didron at Mount Athos contained not only a long series of rigid technical instructions, but also an enumeration of ' Motifs ' of many hundreds of compositions, covering all the accepted themes in the Bible and sacred hagiology. The document, in this form, can be traced to the sixteenth century, but covers a practice extending back many centuries before, as one may see from the persistence of certain types in frescoes and mosaics that antedate the MS.* '

One wonders if any similar guide existed for the use of musicians. We can see that there certainly was a stockpot of ' ideas '—that is, type-formulae—upon which ' composers ' drew, but the results were naturally far freer and more varied than the repetitions which we find, let us say, in some of the Ravenna mosaics!

Apart from the piecing together of different fragments, there is another procedure which Ferretti calls ' *melodie-typo* ', known also in Greek as ' *heirmoi* ', and in Syrian as ' *risqolo* '.

' A heirmos is a chant, verses, quasi verses, or tolerable rhythmic prose, which can be adapted without modification, or with alterations of slight detail, to a number of texts provided they be of like division. . . . The hymns, however, are not at all the only pieces of Western Chant that present this feature. Among the antiphons of the Office there are numerous melodies that recur, on different texts, many times in the antiphonary†.'

* *The Painter in History*, pp. 34-5. Ernest H. Short. (Philip Allan.)
† *Religious Music*, p. 29. R. A. Grain. (Sands.)

Dom Mocquereau, in a study of the intonation of an antiphon of the first mode (type, *Tu es pastor ovium*) has called attention to no less than seventy-five examples in a single MS, the comparison of which is very instructive.

I have chosen thirteen of the most interesting examples of these, selecting the ones which most clearly show with what wonderful resource and variety the composers treated the type-antiphon, and the comparison of the examples gives a remarkable insight into the methods of these unknown composers.

The Type Antiphon 1F

(*Key-signature* for all examples—C : d.)

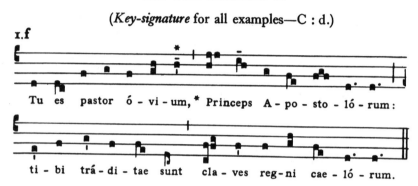

(Thou art shepherd of the sheep, the Prince of the Apostles: to thee have been given the keys of the Kingdom of Heaven.)

This example may be taken for the type. The mode is well marked in the intonation, showing the final and dominant (*).

(Because thou hast done it to one of the least of mine, thou hast done it to Me, saith the Lord.)

The dominant is avoided in the intonation and only appears as a passing note. The compass is only of four notes, emphasizing naïvely the 'least of my little ones'.

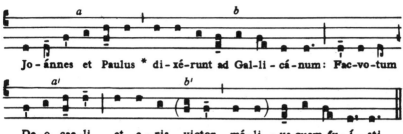

Jo-ánnes et Paulus * di-xé-runt ad Gal-li-cá-num: Fac-vo-tum
De-o cae-li,   et e-ris   victor mé-li - us quam fu- í - sti.

(John and Paul said to Gallicanus: ' Make a vow to the God of Heaven, and thou shalt be the victor better than heretofore.')

The intonation as in *Tu es pastor*, but note in this example the balance of phrases creating the form a-b-a¹-b¹, with a skilful insertion of notes in b¹ to accommodate the extra words.

Pu-éllae sal-ta-ni * im-pe-rá-vit ma - ter: Ni-hil á - li-ud
pe-tas ni - se ca-put Jo - án - nes.

(To the girl as she danced her mother commanded: ' Do thou ask nothing but the head of John.')

Intonation as in *Tu es pastor*. There is a cruel decisiveness in Herodias' command to Salome which is well expressed in its syllabic treatment.

Fulcí - te me fló-ri-bus,* sti-pá-te me ma - lis, qui - a
a - mó - re língue-o.

(Stay me with flowers, sustain me with fruits, for I am faint with love.)

The exquisite words may be said to force the lovely melodic sequence on the music. Notice the tender effect of the accidental B♭, and the beautiful last phrase, ' *amore langueo* ', in which two notes to each of the three vowels bring a feeling of human passion into the music, piercing through the mystical sense of the words.

Qui vult ve - ní - re post me, * áb - ne - get se - met ípsum,

et tollat crucem su - am, et sequá - tur-me.

(He who will follow after Me, let him deny himself, and take up his cross, and follow Me.)

We recover the typical intonation: but notice the well-placed B♭ giving force to ' *abneget* ' (' deny ').

A - men, a - men di - co vo-bis: * í - te - rum vi - dé - bo vos,

et gaudé - bit cor vestrum, et gáudi - um vestrum nemo tollet

a vo - bis, al - le - lú - ia.

(Verily, verily, I say unto you: I shall see you again, and your heart shall be glad, and your gladness shall no one take from you, alleluia.)

What a feeling for words these old Gregorianists had! The two notes for the second syllable of the repeated ' Amen ' are exactly right in reinforcing the word. So is the neumatic group at ' *iterum* ' (' again '). There is a feeling of development in the semi-sequential ' *et gaudium vestrum—nemo tollet a vobis* '.

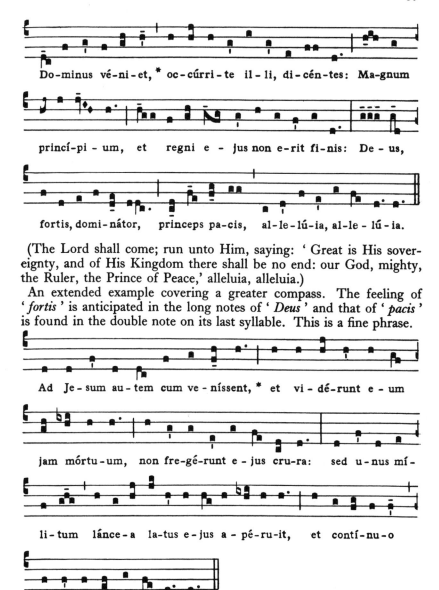

Do-minus vé-ni-et, * oc-cúrri-te il-li, di-cén-tes: Ma-gnum

princí-pi - um, et regni e - Jus non e-rit fi-nis: De - us,

fortis, domi-nátor, princeps pa-cis, al-le-lú-ia, al-le - lú-ia.

(The Lord shall come; run unto Him, saying: ' Great is His sover-
eignty, and of His Kingdom there shall be no end: our God, mighty,
the Ruler, the Prince of Peace,' alleluia, alleluia.)

An extended example covering a greater compass. The feeling of
' fortis ' is anticipated in the long notes of ' Deus ' and that of ' pacis '
is found in the double note on its last syllable. This is a fine phrase.

Ad Je-sum au-tem cum ve - níssent, * et vi - dé-runt e - um

jam mórtu-um, non fre-gé-runt e - jus cru-ra: sed u-nus mí-

li-tum lánce-a la-tus e-jus a - pé-ru-it, et contí-nu-o

ex-í-vit sanguis et aqua.

(But when they had come to Jesus, and saw Him already dead, they
did not break His legs: but one of the soldiers pierced His side with a
lance, and forthwith there came out blood and water.)

A modern example (1670) with the compass extended further by one
note. Not very interesting.

Virgo prudentís - si - ma, * quo progré - de - ris, qua-si

au - ró - ra val-de rú-ti - lans? Fí-li - a Si-on, to - ta for-

mó-sa et su-á-vis es: pulchra ut lu - na, e - lé - cta ut sol.

(Virgin most prudent, whither goest thou, like the dawn brightly shining? Daughter of Sion, thou art all lovely and fair, beautiful as the moon, choice as the sun.)

This example shows a beautiful treatment of words, particularly at the tender phrase '*formosa et suavis es*'. The touching of the C on the vowel 'a' of '*suavis*' ('lovely') at this point just hits off the feeling of the word.

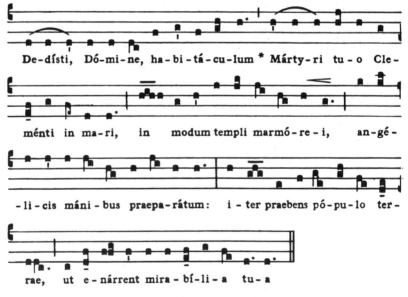

De-dísti, Dó-mi-ne, ha-bi-tá-cu-lum * Márty-ri tu-o Cle-

ménti in ma-ri, in modum templi marmó-re-i, an-gé-

-li-cis máni-bus praepa-rátum: i - ter praebens pó-pu-lo ter-

rae, ut e-nárrent mira-bí-li-a tu-a

(Thou didst give, O Lord, to thy Martyr Clement an habitation in the sea, like unto a marble temple made ready by the hands of angels, and didst make a way for the people of the land, that they might declare thy marvellous works.)

The compass has now grown to over an octave from the original five-note compass of *Tu es pastor*. The climax at '*angelicis*' brings out well the point of the text that the temple of marble built for the Martyr was fashioned by Angels.

Na-tí-vi-tas tu-a, * De-i Gé-nitrix Vir-go, gáudi-um an nunti á-vit u-ni-vér-so mundo: ex te e-nim ortus est Sol justí-ti-ae, Christus De-us no-ster: qui solvens ma-le-dicti-ónem, de-dit bene-dicti-ónem: et confúndens mortem, do-ná-vit no-bis vi-tem sempi-térnam.

(Thy birth, O Virgin Mother of God, announced joy to the whole world: for from thee arose the Sun of Justice, Christ our God: Who unbinding the curse, gave blessing: and vanquishing death, gave unto us life everlasting.)

This example is a marvel of organization and growth. It falls into two sections, '*qui solvens*' being the recapitulation of '*nativitas*'. There are five identical cadences, and two repetitions of the downward figure at (*annuntia*)*vit*, which bind the piece together.

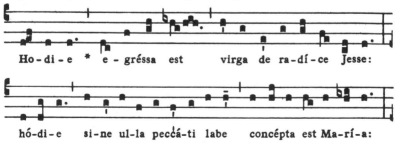

Ho-di-e * e-gréssa est virga de ra-dí-ce Jesse: hó-di-e si-ne ul-la peccá-ti labe concépta est Ma-rí-a:

hó - di - e   contrítum est ab e - a   ca - put serpéntis anti -

qui, al - le - lú - ia.

(To-day there has come forth a shoot from the stem of Jesse: to-day without any stain of sin has Mary been conceived: to-day has the serpent of old been bruised by her.)

Notice the development of the phrase to the word ' *hodie* ' (' to-day '). At its first repetition it rises a note to the interval of a fourth, at the next repetition it rises a fifth with the B^b as a passing note. After the tender cadence at ' *Maria* ' anticipating the group at the ' *hodie* ' following, comes the climatic group ' *contritum et ab ea* '. (Compare this treatment of the three ' *hodie* ' with those in the antiphon ' *Tribus miraculis* ' (p. 99) and with those in the Magnificat antiphon at the 2nd Vespers of Christmas.)

An examination of only thirteen out of the possible examples of one type antiphon must surely convince the reader that these composers had a truly sensitive feeling for words and a great power, within the limited sphere in which they worked, of musical development. It is significant that the modern example is the least striking. Another art had been lost by the end of the eleventh century.

CHAPTER V

THE DRAMATIC IN PLAINCHANT

I. Dramatic Dialogue and Pictures

In one of her charming books, Vernon Lee says that her Catholic friends always used to deprecate those things that most appealed to her in the services of the Church at which she was present. Perhaps she was referring to some such dramatic aspects of, or accompaniments to, the Liturgy as clouds of incense floating heavenwards, the Cross borne high above the heads of the people, the first verse of the *Adeste Fideles* at Midnight Mass, or some moments of the ceremonies of Holy Week. Such things, accidentally dramatic and non-essential, naturally impress the non-Catholic more forcibly than those who are well accustomed to them. But I have often felt that the Liturgy would be more reverently carried out were it remembered that the liturgical drama is indeed acted, the solemn ' ballet ' of the Mass danced, in the sanctuary*.

The Gregorian chant was the music drama of the Middle Ages, and the Church is the mother not only of modern music, but also of the modern theatre, however much she may now disown her children, however large the gulf which, alas! now separates her from them: for it would be idle to pretend that the divorce is not complete. It is a tragic fact that to-day the Church has lost the artist, and the artist has lost his faith.

Hence it comes about that it is largely forgotten by those Catholics who cry out against the performance of mystery plays in our cathedrals and churches that these plays were enormously popular with our forefathers and were only banished when things had gone a bit too far. Once the procession went from the Church into the market-place the Church lost control of the drama. That reform was indeed due the following extract from Henderson's *Forerunners of the Italian Opera*† abundantly shows:

' The feast of the ass, celebrated on January 14th every year at *Beauvais*, was an excellent example of this sort of (profane) ceremony. This was a representation of the flight into Egypt. A beautiful young woman, carrying in her arms an infant gorgeously dressed, was mounted on an ass. Then she moved with a procession from the Cathedral to the church of *St Etienne*. The procession marched into the choir, while the girl, still riding the ass, took a position in front of the altar. Then the Mass was celebrated, and at the end of each part the words " *Hin han* " were chanted in imitation of the braying beast. The officiating priest,

* See the chapter on ' Dramatic Elements of the Liturgy ' (Vol. I) in Karl Young's magnificent work *The Drama of the Medieval Church* (2 vols., Oxford Press, 1933).

† *Forerunners of the Italian Opera.* W. J. Henderson. (Murray.)

instead of chanting the " *Ite missa est* ", invited the congregation to join in imitating the bray*.'

And in 1541 a Canon of *San Domenico di Sesso* wrote a ' *Sacra Rappresentazione* ' called ' The Creation of Adam ', in which he appeared, most realistically, in the title rôle, with great success!

Abuse of a thing, however, is no reason for its expulsion, but for its purification. There are indeed many lovely things that were lost at the time of the Reformation—or which were obscured by what has been called the ' glaring façade of the Counter-Reformation '—that still await restoration when Catholics show more regard for their rich heritage.

It is a bad state of things when one is solemnly informed, as I have sometimes been, that carol-singing is Protestant and, if done at all, should certainly not be done in church! The authorities at Westminster Cathedral do not, happily, take this unhistorical view, and the carol-singing during Epiphany is one of the most lovely musical experiences of the year, drawing many to the great church who do not normally enter it, but whose hearts are touched by these exquisitely rendered religious songs of the people.

Now everything in the Roman Liturgy is eminently practical and only, as I have said, accidentally dramatic. Nevertheless, there is no reason why we should deprecate a consciously beautiful, a controlled dramatic, performance of ritual gestures, words, and music.

We may not, as David did, dance furiously before the altar, but the ceremonies of High Mass do indeed partake of the nature of a solemn ritual dance.

Aesthetic appreciation of the part we are called upon to play could only hurt us, only strike a false note, were there no true faith behind our actions, no controlling discipline, no sense of the holy; if it were art for man's and not for God's sake.

To the Catholic, performances of the *Miracle* or of *Parsifal* are distasteful precisely because they are purely theatrical, and the purely theatrical is poles apart from the religious-dramatic.

We certainly do not want our sanctuaries to be invaded by ecclesiastical mannequins, or aesthetic effeminates: but we do need those who minister there, in whatever capacity, to be filled with a sense of the splendour, the beauty, the dramatic appropriateness of what they are doing.

There is, of course, a danger, Dr Guardini again warns us, that ' in the liturgical sphere aestheticism may spread; that the Liturgy will first be the subject of general eulogy, then gradually its various treasures will be estimated at their aesthetic value, until finally the sacred beauty of the House of God comes to provide a delicate morsel for the connoisseur. Until, that is, the " house of prayer " becomes once more,

---

* See also the *Drama of the Medieval Church*, vol. I, p. 105. Karl Young (Oxford Press).

in a different way, a " den of thieves ". But for the sake of Him who dwells there, and for that of our own souls, this must not be tolerated.' The Abbot of *Marialaach* rightly remarks in this connection: ' I stress the point that the Liturgy has *developed* into a work of art; it was not deliberately formed as such by the Church. The Liturgy bore within itself so much of the seed of beauty that it was of itself bound to flower ultimately. But the internal principle which controlled the form of that flowering was the essence of Christianity*.'

And Abbot Vonier writes: ' The liturgical movement is above all things a renovation among us of the art of celebrating the Christian Feasts and consequently of presenting to the people the mysteries of God in a splendid fashion. The parish priest who gives to his people a great Christmas, a glorious Easter, a splendid Corpus Christi festivity, is a first-class liturgist, though he may press into service methods old and new. The matter of supreme importance is this, that the faithful should know the meaning of each Feast as that Feast comes along in its turn; the theology of the celebration ought to enter their minds by every one of their senses: they ought to see the divine Babe, they ought to hear the Canticles of Bethlehem; the incense of the altar ought to remind them of the gifts of the Magi. . . .† '

This long preamble leads up to the main point of the chapter, the place of the dramatic—not, I must again safeguard myself by saying—not the transpontine or the theatrical—in plainchant. It is surely wrong, from every point of view, that the Communion depicting the Miracle at Cana, for example, should be sung throughout in one tone of voice. This piece of plainchant (see p. 72) is sheer programme music, and the picture it paints so vividly should be made clear to the listening congregation. The remoteness of the Liturgy from the average emotional attitude must not be allowed to become too great.

Words that are quoted, as, for instance, the words of Our Lord, of Rachel weeping for her children (p. 69), should not be run, as one colour into another, into the sentences which precede and follow them, but should be clearly differentiated from these. The music (of the Chant) says the Pian decree, is to add greater efficacy to the words, but this will not be done by interpreting it in one uniform tone of voice, but by using every *legitimate* means to that end, and therefore, when indicated, a dramatic means.

What will become, exclaims the terrified conventionalist, the liturgical fanatic, of the true nature of the Chant, which is to be absolutely calm, grave, smooth.

I deny that the true spirit of the Chant would be in any way violated: on the contrary, I believe that it would more fully appear, and appeal

* Herwegen, *Das Kunstprinzip der Liturgie*, p. 18. (Paderborn, 1916.)

† ' The Doctrinal Power of the Liturgy of the Catholic Church.' Abbot Vonier. (*Clergy Review*, January 1935.)

to many whom the grey monotony which informs the chant so often, at present, repels.

Are the seasons, the feasts of the Church, all of the same colour and the same in spirit? We know how the Church sometimes weeps, sometimes rejoices, and what a variety of moods she employs in the Liturgy. The celebrating priest issues forth in black and in red, in purple, in green, in white and in gold, his assistants and the altar in harmony with him. Surely the music alone is not to sound always and ever precisely the same!

Yet to utter the word dramatic is enough to call forth censure, so timidly puritan have we become, so terrified of any artistic risk, so lacking in imagination.

The medium, whatever it is, must always be respected and not strained. The musician does not write orchestrally for the string quartet, or, if he does, he is no musician. The *lieder* singer does not use operatic gestures on the concert platform, or, if she does, she is no artist. The true musician, the true artist, keeps always within the confines of his chosen medium; but how wide the range is may be seen by comparing a Haydn quartet with a Bartok quartet, a folk-song with a song of Wolf; and in plainchant—in which exists a far richer emotional world than we have been led to suspect—by comparing the tender little motet *Anima Christi* with the terrible utterance of the responsory *Tenebrae facti sunt*, and recalling all that lies in between.

We are to be concerned here with the question of dramatic dialogues and scenes, and not with single words or phrases, which will be spoken of in the next chapter.

Examine the following antiphon (Quinquagesima Sunday).

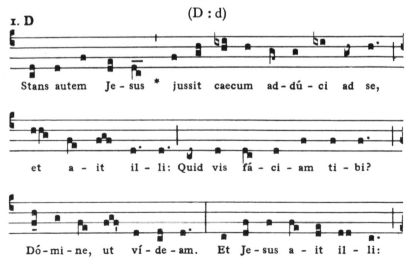

1. D   (D : d)

Stans autem   Je - sus * jussit caecum ad - dú - ci ad se,

et   a - it   il - li: Quid vis fá - ci - am ti - bi?

Dó - mi - ne, ut   ví - de - am.   Et Je - sus a - it il - li:

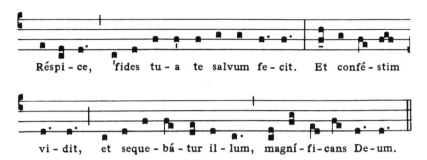

Réspi - ce,   'fides tu - a   te salvum fe - cit.   Et confé - stim

vi - dit,   et seque - bá - tur il - lum, magní - fi - cans De - um.

(But Jesus stood and bade them bring the blind man to Him, and said
to him: ' What wouldst thou that I should do to thee? ' ' Lord, that
I may see.' And Jesus said to him: ' Look about thee, thy faith hath
made thee sound.' And straightway he saw, and followed Him,
glorifying God.)

If it is sung through without any differentiation of tone, the whole
lesson of the antiphon is lost, the picture dimmed.

Put the text into dramatic form:

Narrator. *Stans autem Jesus jussit caecum adduci ad se et ait illi:*
Jesus. *Quid vis faciam tibi?*
Blind man. *Domine ut videam.*
Narrator. *Jesus ait illi:*
Jesus. *Respice, fides tua te salvum fecit.*
Narrator (or chorus). *Et confestim vidit et sequebatur illum magnificans
Deum.*

and immediately a grey monotone is seen to be impossible.

The music must, therefore, be sung either with varying degrees of
tonal power, e.g., by a division of the choir, or—and much more satis-
factorily where possible and practicable—by allotting the different
parts to different voices, as suggested above: provided that the announc-
ing of the antiphon is made in the usual traditional manner, the rhythmic
flow is not broken and the music is not *dramatised* though sung in
dramatic form. The Narrator will not indeed give himself the licence
of the Narrator in the Bach Passions, but rather model himself, as also
the others, on the style used for the plainchant ' Passions '.

There need be no set method of treatment so long as the great aim of
thinking the words before singing them, and in singing them enhancing
and projecting their meaning, is kept to the fore.

Thus the following Communion (St John Apostle and Evangelist) is
obviously not susceptible of a dialogue treatment:

Narrator. *Exit sermo inter fratres, quod discipulus ille non moritur et
non dixit Jesus:*
Jesus. *Non moritur:*
Narrator. *Sed:*

Jesus. *Sic eum volo manere, donec veniam.*
for the words of Our Lord are merely being quoted. But in the next
example (Feast of Holy Family) a division between men and boys
might effectively be made.

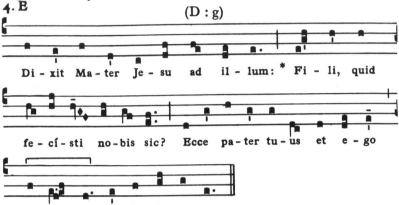

(The Mother of Jesus said to Him: ' Son, why hast Thou dealt thus
with us? Behold, Thy father and I sought Thee sorrowing.')
(Notice the illustrative neumatic group at the word ' *dolentes* '*:
a slight *rallentando* should be made at this point, besides the usual one
at ' *quaerebamus te* '.)
In the example below (ninth Sunday after Pentecost) a few voices
should sing as far as ' *eo* ': and then the remainder of the choir very
softly and slowly end with the ' *dicit Dominus* ', without stressing the
tonic syllable of the last word, which should be short and light.

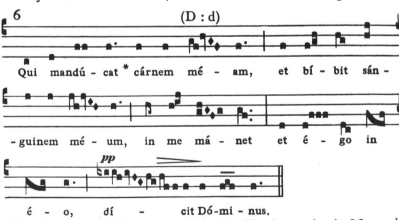

(He who eats My Flesh, and drinks My Blood, remains in Me, and
I in him, saith the Lord.)

* Here, and very often elsewhere, the *quilisma* is used as an expressive device.

The Magi should be represented by a small division of the choir in the antiphon below (1st Vespers of the Epiphany).

The warning given on page 27 should be taken note of in the singing of this antiphon, for the same phrase as that set to *fundatus enim* is found again here at the words *hoc signum magni*.

8. G   (D : g)

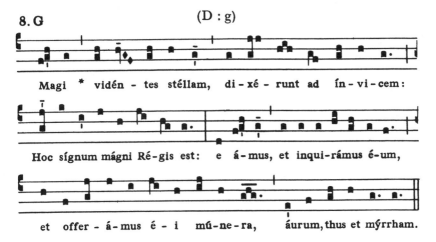

(The Wise Men saw the Star, and said one to another: This is the sign of the great King: let us go, and seek after Him, and offer Him gifts, gold, frankincense, and myrrh.')

7   (B♭ : c)

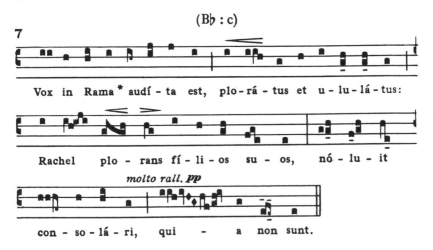

(A cry has been heard in Rama, weeping and lamentation: Rachel, weeping for her children, has refused consolation, because they are not.)

F

In the Communion of the Mass for the Holy Innocents* we are given a tragic picture of Rachel weeping for her children, the emotion ever growing through the doubled note at *ploratus*, and the sorrow-laden figures at *ululatus* and *plorans*. The phrase at '*noluit*' should be sung with full appreciation of its beautiful shape; notice how the lowest note of each group falls each time, while the repeated B flats intensify the feeling of grief—until the heartbreaking '*Quia non sunt*', to be sung with a big *rallentando* and decreasing tone, the '*non sunt*' very soft. The tone throughout should be dark and viola-like.

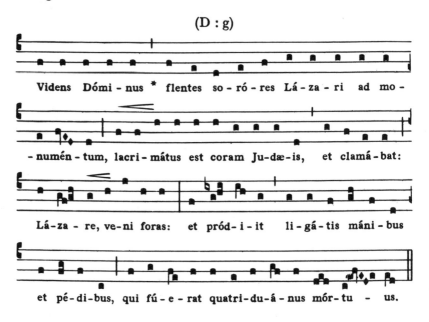

(When the Lord saw the sisters of Lazarus weeping at his tomb, He shed tears before the Jews, and cried: 'Lazarus, come forth.' And he who had been dead four days came forth with his hands and his feet bound.)

The weeping of Lazarus' sisters at his tomb and the sorrow of Christ are illustrated by the opening phrase, '*Videns Dominus*' (sixth Feria after fourth Sunday of Lent), the pulsations of which are twice repeated, and each time at a higher pitch, reaching a climax on the stressed syllable of '*lacrimatus*'. The command to Lazarus to come forth, with the climax on the word '*veni*', is most dramatically expressed by its economical musical phrase. These words should undoubtedly be sung by a solo voice.

* The plain Vatican text is used for the two examples above and that on p. 72.

(Alleluia. The flowers have appeared in our land. Alleluia. The voice of the turtle-dove has been heard.)

A real feeling of spring is apparent in the *Alleluia* for Easter-time in the Feast of the Apparition of the Blessed Virgin Mary Immaculate. It is especially brought out by the extended phrase at ' *apparuerunt* ', in which the flowers burst joyfully into bloom. The versicle of an *Alleluia*, as Vincent D'Indy has pointed out, is dramatic, but the *jubilus* at its last syllable—repeating the same theme as is associated with the final syllable of the *Alleluia*—is symphonic. A *crescendo*, and not a

softening, is indicated at the echo-phrase of ' *apparuerunt* '. In the
lovely *Alleluia* outside Easter-time, the descending notes before the
quarter-bar of the neumatic group of the *jubilus* are further developed at
' *tur* ' *(turis)* to imitate the voice of the dove that is heard in the land.
To bring out the idea of call answering call, make the echo-repetition
soft. We watch the bird climb into the air and fly away at the concluding
phrase *(est)* repeated from the *Alleluia.*

6   (D : g)

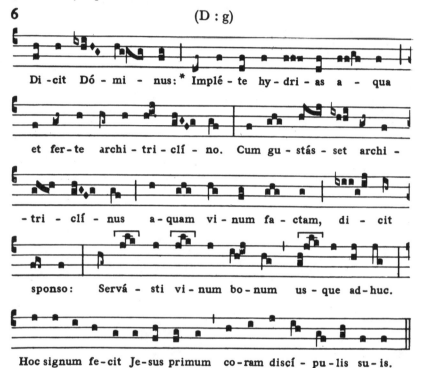

Di -cit Dó - mi - nus: * Implé - te hy - dri - as a - qua

et fer - te archi - tri - clí - no. Cum gu - stás - set archi -

- tri - clí - nus a - quam vi - num fa - ctam, di - cit

sponso: Servá - sti vi - num bo - num us - que ad - huc.

Hoc signum fe - cit Je - sus primum co - ram discí - pu - lis su - is.

(The Lord saith: ' Fill the water-jars with water, and take them to the
president of the feast.' When the president had tasted the water made
wine, he saith to the bridegroom: ' Thou hast kept the good wine till
now '. This was the first sign which Jesus did before His disciples.)

The Communion illustrating the changing of the water into wine is
the most perfectly organized of all these dramatic pictures. Our Lord's
words are given a quiet confidence by the twofold repetition of the
figure at *im(plete)*. When the water has been miraculously changed
the delight of the grateful steward knows no bounds, and finds expression in the joyous phrase, also twice repeated, at ' *servasti* '. Finally, to
round off the picture, comes the sudden drop into quiet, recitative
' This first miracle did Jesus. . . .'

The full beauty of this remarkable piece will only be felt when the tone levels have been most carefully rehearsed. ' *Hoc signum* ' should be sung very quietly, lightly and faster than the previous section.

(It may be thought that the intoning of the Magnificat (or other doubled antiphons) is likely to present a difficulty to the realization of the scheme set out above, but the voice or voices allotted to the opening phrase will simply take up their part after the asterisk and begin the antiphon at the end of the canticle (or psalm), according to custom.)

CHAPTER VI

THE DRAMATIC IN PLAINCHANT

II. WORD PAINTING

' Now the justness of Wolf's accentuation, the way in which the melodic accent coincides with the verbal, is wonderful.' So writes Ernest Newman in his study of Hugo Wolf*: and it is the loving care for words, the effort to find, with such slender means, a real tonal embodiment of the text and its just accentuation that distinguishes plainchant.

I have already tried to show in Chapter IV what an insight into the methods of the Gregorian composers may be gained by a comparison of thirteen settings of the same type-antiphon. The alterations and modifications in each one are caused by the differing texts, and it is patent that if the treatment of words is important in Wolf *lieder*, it is even more so the case in plainchant with its two sole lines of appeal, the literary and the melodic.

There are some examples of plainchant in the Roman Gradual where the desire for display is more evident than the selfless beauty usually characteristic of the Chant. I imagine that the singers shown in the mosaics of the Church of SS Cosmas and Damien, to whom I have before referred, would have revelled in just such an opportunity to show off their virtuosity as the piece of music given below affords in several of its phrases: and when Erasmus spoke in scorn of some singers as ' a set of creatures who should be bewailing their sins think to please God by gurgling in their throats ', it might well have been this kind of thing he had in mind.

℣. Con - fi - ti - án - - - - - tur

Dó - mi - no

Very different is the Gregorianists' prevailing desire to find a real tonal embodiment for the words, and, at the same time, give the voice legitimate opportunities of expression.

* *Hugo Wolf*, by Ernest Newman, p. 160. (Methuen.)

'A choir that hopes to interest its hearers must first interest itself,' and the lack of feeling for words is undoubtedly what makes so much solo and choral singing sound monotonous.

Enough, surely, has now been written about the rhythm of plainchant; indeed, so much so that the literary aspect of the Chant has been more or less overlooked. But this, instead of being the last thing to teach a choir, should be one of the first. Shakespeare's plays reflect the speech of his day—a beautiful utterance: and playwrights to-day reflect our lazy habits of speech and scamped diction: but Latin, gloriously dead language, is now superior to the changing fortunes of different ages, and the choirmaster should do all possible to get his people to love and understand it. Even if the words are not yet comprehended, how beautiful is the sound alone of such phrases as these:

Fulcite me floribus, stipate me malis, quia amore langueo.
(Stay me with flowers, sustain me with fruits, for I am faint with love.)
Tristis est anima mea usque ad mortem.
(My soul is sorrowful even unto death.)
O clemens, O pia, O dulcis Virgo Maria.
(O clement, O loving, O sweet Virgin Mary.)

And as beautifully as these sentences are when said so should they be phrased and sung, every word reaching the hearers. We must also never allow ourselves to forget the words of Benedict XIV: 'First it is requisite that the words which are being sung shall be clearly and rightly understood.'

Now throughout plainchant there are clear instances of word painting, often quite simple, usually exquisitely appropriate, that form tonal illustrations and pictures which must be used and appreciated in building up vital interpretations*.

I well remember spending an afternoon in Rome accompanying a great expert (of the Solesmes school) in plainchant in a number of songs ranging from Schubert to Moussorgsky. I was surprised to hear that he sang every one in precisely the same manner and without any real savouring of the words. That is, indeed, the phrase. The words must be savoured. If they are to be heard and appreciated they must be thought and felt.

The examples that follow are chosen on no determined plan—this is not a scientific work—but for their special suitability in illustrating the thesis of this chapter. And they represent a mere fraction of those I have noted down from time to time.

The methods of the Gregorian composer will be seen not to be essentially unlike those of Bach. Sometimes a single word receives clear illustration, or the word, as it were, throws just a shadow over the music; and at other times the spirit of one word, or sentence, informs the whole passage.

* The Byzantine melodies have the same illustrative character. See Egon Wellesz' introductory remarks to *Trésor de Musique Byzantine*. (Lyrebird Press, 1934.)

I cannot too strongly emphasize that in performance none of the words below should stand out like neon-electric signs in the prevailing darkness, but that they should always have a proper relation to the whole piece. That will be the guarantee of a true artistic treatment.

In Vespers of the first Sunday in Advent there is that sudden premature cry of joy in the second antiphon, as if the Church could not even wait until *Laetare* Sunday to utter her gladness at the approaching birth of the Saviour*.

Ju-cun-dá - re *

(Rejoice (O daughter of Sion).)

' *Jucunditatem* ' receives something of the same, though less exuberant, treatment in the Communion of the Mass for the second Sunday in Advent.

ju - cun - di - tá - tem,

(see the) joyfulness (which will come to thee).

But it is after Christmas that there comes the most thrilling burst of joy (Offertory, second Sunday after Epiphany), covering the unusually large compass of a 12th in its great arches of melody.

- te   Dé - o

(Shout with joy to God, (all ye earth).)

The example of a phrase from Bach's Church Cantata ' *Es ist Genug* ', illustrative of joy, given here for comparison, may well send my reader to the two absorbing chapters in the second volume of Schweitzer's great book on Bach, in which he writes about the musical language of

---

* I imagine that by now the reader will have no difficulty in reading the musical examples, so that no more aids need be given!

the Chorales and the Church Cantatas, and shows the way in which Bach used motives of joy and sorrow, ' step ' motives, and various pictorial themes.

with joy————— I   bid the world fare-well;   it is   e - nough.

Plainchant also has a rudimentary and unsystematized tonal language which is wonderfully expressive considering the one dimension in which it moves. Already we have had examples of motives of joy (to say nothing of other motives to be found in previous chapters), and we can discover ' step ' and ' speaking ' motives as well as most of the others classified by Schweitzer*.

Step Motives of Ascent and Descent

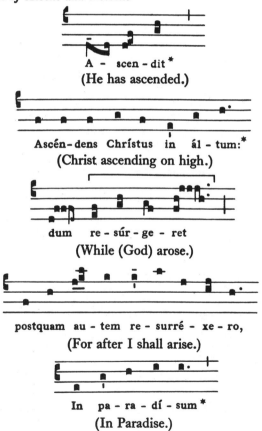

A - scen - dit *
(He has ascended.)

Ascén-dens Chrístus in   ál - tum:*
(Christ ascending on high.)

dum   re - súr - ge - ret
(While (God) arose.)

postquam au - tem re - surré - xe - ro,
(For after I shall arise.)

In   pa - ra - dí - sum *
(In Paradise.)

* *J. S. Bach*, by Albert Schweitzer (translated by Ernest Newman), Chapters XXII-XXIII. (Black.)

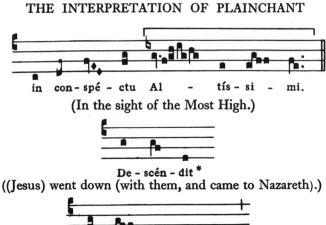

in con - spé - ctu Al   -   tís - si - mi.
(In the sight of the Most High.)

De - scén - dit *
((Jesus) went down (with them, and came to Nazareth).)

De - scén - dit Jé - sus *
(Jesus went down (with them).)

Mí - cha - el de - scen - dé - bat * de caé - lo.

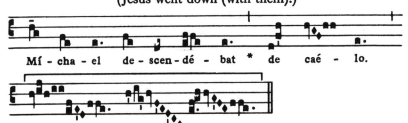

(Michael was descending from Heaven.)

Motives of Praise

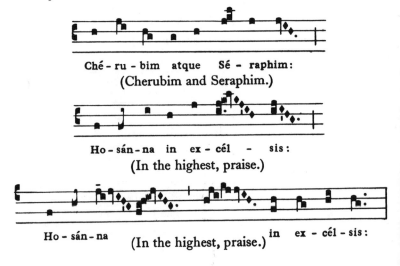

Ché - ru - bim atque Sé - raphim:
(Cherubim and Seraphim.)

Ho - sán - na in ex - cél - sis:
(In the highest, praise.)

Ho - sán - na   (In the highest, praise.)   in ex - cél - sis:

3

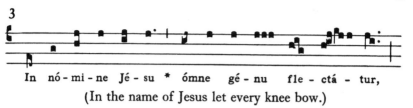

In nó - mi - ne Jé - su * ómne gé - nu fle - ctá - tur,

(In the name of Jesus let every knee bow.)

Quite possibly there was no intention to find a tonal equivalent for ' *flectatur* '—one must not be fanciful—but we should take notice of the shape of the neum on the first syllable of the word and at least keep the picture in mind.

' *Speaking* ' *Motives*

The ' *clamor* ', the cry in the night, is vividly limned by a simple phrase in the Communion for the Common of Virgins.

5

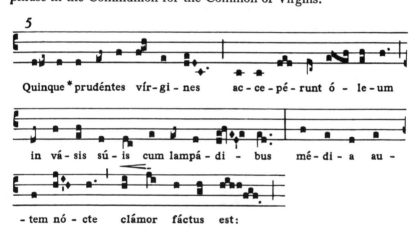

Quinque * prudéntes vír-gi - nes ac - ce - pé - runt ó - le - um

in vá - sis sú - is cum lampá - di - bus mé - di - a au -

- tem nó - cte clámor fáctus est:

(The five prudent virgins took oil in their vessels with the lamps: and in the middle of the night there was a cry ('Lo! the bridegroom comes').)

After the supplicating opening of the magnificent Tract that we sing in Lent, how dramatic is the high-flung cry of ' *Adjuva nos* '. And the twofold repetition at (*invo*)*ca-vi* (*Domin*)*um* in the Introit for Septuagesima Sunday gives great force to the call of the troubled soul to God.

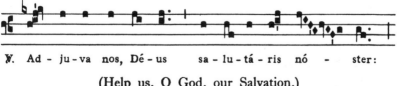

℣. Ad - ju - va nos, Dé - us sa - lu - tá - ris nó - ster:

(Help us, O God, our Salvation.)

in - vo - cá - vi   Dó - mi - num,

(I have called upon the Lord.)

How beautifully placed is ' *Deus* ' in the following antiphon (Conversion of St Paul), bringing out the force of the words that ' I planted, Apollo watered (but) God gave the increase '.

8. G

E - go plantá - vi, * Apól - lo ri - gávit: De - us   au - tem

increméntum   de - dit, al - le - lú - ia.

(I sowed the seed, Apollo hath watered it: but God hath given the increase, alleluia.)

These key-words in all instances should receive a slight or considerable stress, the phrases in which they occur degrees of *rallentando* decided according to the context. Thus *surge* (Communion of the Second Sunday in Advent), after a rather quick, moderately soft beginning, should be sung slowly with full tone.

2

Je - rú - sa - lem * súrge,   et   sta   in   ex - cél - so :

(Jerusalem, arise, and stand up on high.)

The well-worn formula (compare the third Antiphon at first Vespers of the Holy Rosary) with which the next example begins, adapts itself well to a ' blowing up ' on the trumpet. (Fourth Sunday in Advent.)

1.g

Ca - ni - te   tú - ba * in   Sí - on,

(Sing to the trumpet in Sion (because the day is near).)

And the last syllable of *gloriae* is also full of the sound of the trumpet.
(Vigil of the Nativity: Offertory.)

2

Tol - li - te * pór - tas,   prín - ci - pes, vé - - stras:

et e - le - vá - - mi - ni, pór   tae ae - ter - ná - les,

et in-tro-í - bit   Rex gló - ri - ae.

(Lift up your gates, O ye princes: and be ye lifted up, ye everlasting
doors, and the King of glory shall come in.)
The following three examples of a resounding ' Hosanna ', a call on
the shepherd's pipe (the end of this antiphon should be soft and most
tender), and the martyr Agnes stretching out her hands to God,
illustrate how well the word colours the formula or intonation.

7

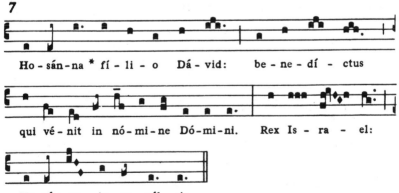

Ho - sán - na * fí - li - o Dá - vid: be - ne - dí - ctus

qui vé - nit in nó - mi - ne Dó - mi - ni.   Rex Is - ra - el:

Ho - sán - na   in ex - cél - sis.

(Hosanna to the Son of David: Blessed is He that cometh in the name
of the Lord, the King of Israel: Hosanna in the highest.)

7. d

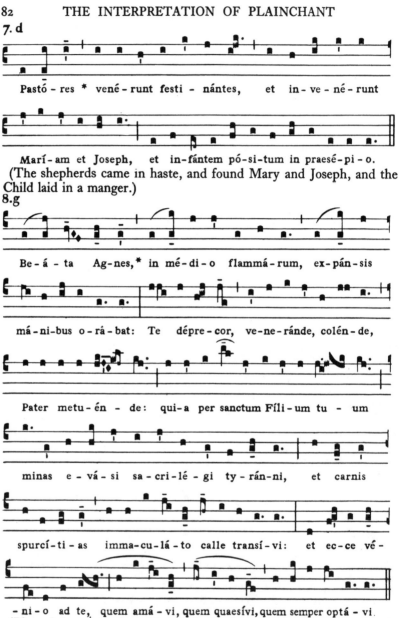

Pastó - res * vené - runt festi - nántes,   et in - ve - né - runt

Marí - am et Joseph,   et in-fántem pó-si-tum in praesé-pi-o.

(The shepherds came in haste, and found Mary and Joseph, and the Child laid in a manger.)

8. g

Be - á - ta   Ag-nes,* in mé-di-o   flammá-rum,   ex-pán-sis

má-ni-bus o-rá-bat: Te   dépre-cor, ve-ne-ránde, colén-de,

Pater metu-én - de: qui-a per sanctum Fíli-um tu - um

minas   e - vá - si   sa - cri-lé - gi ty - rán-ni,   et   carnis

spurcí-ti - as   imma-cu-lá-to calle transí-vi: et ec-ce vé -

- ni-o ad te, quem amá-vi, quem quaesívi, quem semper optá-vi.

(Blessed Agnes, in the midst of the flames, stretched forth her hands and prayed:" I beseech Thee, most venerable, most worshipful Father to be feared: because through Thy holy Son I have escaped the threats of the impious tyrant, and have passed through the filthiness of the flesh by an immaculate path: and lo! I come to Thee, Whom I have loved, Whom I have sought, Whom I have always hoped for.')

Motives of Grief

I cannot resist quoting two well-known examples from the music of Holy Week, with which I hope to deal as a whole in another book. There is the terrible cry from the Cross in the Responsory ' *Tenebrae factae sunt*', set to a phrase that seems to leap out of the page at one so startling is its melodic elevation. The phrase should be allotted to an experienced tenor voice. The other example is one of the loveliest and most memorable in the whole range of plainchant. Simplicity itself, its few notes bring poignantly to mind the picture of the fall and destruction of Jerusalem foretold in the words spoken by Our Lord at His triumphal entry into the city. ' And when he drew near, seeing the city, He wept over it, saying: " If thou also hadst known, and that in this thy day, the things that are to thy peace: but now they are hidden from thy eyes. For the days shall come upon thee, and thy enemies shall cast a trench about thee and compass thee round, and straiten thee on every side. And beat thee flat to the ground, and thy children who are in thee: and they shall not leave in thee a stone upon a stone: because thou hast not known the time of thy visitation." '

(Jesus cried out with a loud voice: ' My God, why hast Thou forsaken me? ' And bending down His head, He gave up the ghost.)

(Jerusalem, Jerusalem, turn to the Lord thy God.)

In the other ' motives of grief ' assembled below the use of the *quilisma* as a device expressive of sorrow will be noticed at ' *Heu Mihi* ', and ' *(iniquitat)em (meum)*,' in which its repetition intensifies the sense of the words.

(Woe is me.)

(Woe is me.)

(My iniquity.)

In the great Office of Holy Week *quilismas* are especially abundant, as one would expect. It frequently happens that the emotion generated by a word is carried not by the principal accent, but by a secondary accent, or is imported into a succeeding word (*Miserere mei*) or spread over a whole phrase or piece. Thus the whole of the *Alleluia* in the Feast of the Seven Sorrows of Our Blessed Lady is coloured by the poignant emotion of the concluding word of the versicle ' *dolorosa* ', and the descending *neums* of the *jubilus* and in the versicle must take their sad tone from the same passage at the end of the versicle. Here is an example of the necessity of seeing a piece of plainchant in its entirety and not as a series of imperfectly related parts. Notice also the small compass and length of the *Alleluia* itself, where there is so little cause for rejoicing.

(Have mercy on me.)

(Alleluia. There stood holy Mary, Queen of Heaven and Mistress of the world, beside the Cross of our Lord Jesus Christ, sorrowful.)

Other Motives

In the next example (Third Sunday after Epiphany), the emotion generated by *gloriam* flows into the succeeding word (*tuam*).

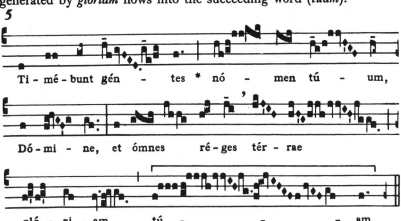

(The nations shall fear Thy name, O Lord, and all the kings of the earth Thy glory.)

G

The agitated coming together of the high priests and the Pharisees is well expressed in the long phrase below.

2

Col - le - gé - runt * pontí - fi - ces et

(The high priests (and the Pharisees) came together.)

The sweep of the angel's wing runs throughout the Offertory of the second *feria* after Easter. Notice the many neumatic groups which break up the words.

8

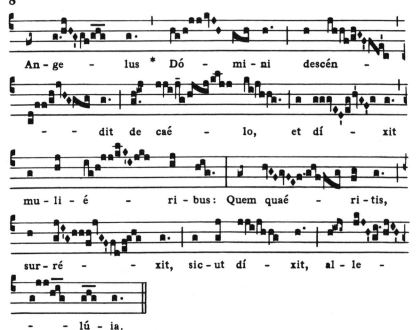

An - ge - lus * Dó - mi - ni descén -

- - dit de caé - lo, et dí - xit

mu - li - é - ri - bus: Quem quaé - ri - tis,

sur - ré - xit, sic - ut dí - xit, al - le -

- - lú - ia.

(An Angel of the Lord came down from Heaven, and said to the women: ' Whom are you seeking? He has risen, as He said ', alleluia.)

Then there is the very different sad sweep of the harp strings of the exiled children of Israel in the Offertory of the Twentieth Sunday after Pentecost. (The first part of the last expressive phrase must be sung as an echo of the previous one, *Sion*, and the end made very slow and sorrowful.)

I

Su - per flú - mi - na * Ba - by - ló -

- nis,   il - lic sé - di - mus,   et   flé - vi - mus,

dum recor - da - ré - mur   tú - i,   Sí - on.

(Over the rivers of Babylon, there sat we down, and wept, while we remembered thee, O Sion.)

There is a charming anticipation of the figuration of Wagner's ' *Waldweben* ' in the Communion of the Mass for the Third Sunday in Lent, phrases to be sung like the dipping flight of a swallow*.

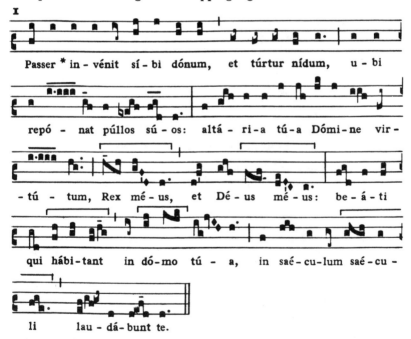

Passer * in - vénit sí - bi dónum,   et túrtur nídum,   u - bi

repó - nat púllos sú - os: altá - ri - a tú - a Dómi - ne   vir -

- tú - tum, Rex mé - us,   et Dé - us mé - us: be - á - ti

qui hábi - tant   in dó - mo tú - a,   in saé - cu - lum saé - cu -

li   lau - dá - bunt te.

(The sparrow hath found her a home, and the turtle-dove a nest where she may lay her young: Thy altars, O Lord of hosts, my King,

* Notice also the points of repose (*re*)*pon*(*at*)-(*vir*)*tut*(*um*): and the carrying out of the main motive (*et turtur nidum*) in the neums put into brackets.

and my God: blessed are they who live in Thy house, they shall praise Thee for ever and ever.)

The descent of the angel and the rolling away of the stone before the tomb of Our Lord are most vividly painted in the Alleluia for the Easter Monday Mass. No one could doubt the aim of the composer to find a tonal equivalent for the words in this example.

(Alleluia. The angel of the Lord came down from heaven: and approaching he rolled back the stone, and sat upon it.)

Finally, analyse carefully the exquisite balance and illustration of the words in the following Communion (St Mark, Evangelist).

- rit, ín - ve - nit: pulsán - ti   a - pe - ri - é - tur,

al - le - - lú - ia.

(Ask, and you shall receive: seek, and you shall find: knock, and it shall be opened to you: for every one who asks, receives, and he who seeks finds: to him who knocks it shall be opened.)

Petite, accipietis; quaerite, invenietis; ever-lengthening phrases. Then the even more extended phrase at *pulsate (aperietur).* In the response there is the same beautiful development through the three sentences— the phrases again ever lengthening—*accepit, invenit, aperietur*—to the climax of joy at the *Alleluia.*

CHAPTER VII

FORM

The most superficial formal analysis of plainchant reveals the presence of a number of formulas which constantly recur in one piece after another so that many plainchant melodies deserve the name of mosaics (' centoni '). These formulas were necessary devices to secure a measure of unity to bind the music together in those early days of composition before thematic invention and development were a conscious process, and one was doubtless expected to help oneself from the traditional stockpot of ideas.

Dom Gajard remarks truly enough that examples of the development of initial themes can be found in plainchant, but are by no means the rule*. But when he remarks that ' the composer followed at his ease the melodic line that his heart dictated. Like the bird flying in space at its will it proceeds without constraint and lets itself go where inspiration carries it ', we can only reply that this popular view of inspiration requires so many qualifications as to be practically valueless.

As has been said so often, ninety-nine per cent of perspiration goes to one per cent of inspiration, and doubtless there were many occasions when the wayward Gregorian bird obstinately refused to fly, and the composer wondered what on earth to do next. Then he would turn to a formula for salvation, with something of the relief of a becalmed yacht that meets the breeze. We may be sure that his task was a hard one and no mere ecstasy of inspiration.

It is, nevertheless, extraordinarily interesting to observe the Gregorian ' composers ' obeying interior artistic impulses in matters of balance and design—and they show an exquisite sense of design—of which, perhaps, they were only faintly aware.

These fragments (or formulas) in these Gregorian mosaics are introduced and combined with such skill that they not only fall naturally upon the ear, never obtruding themselves, but possess a never-failing charm and power of appeal.

Gevaert has noted in this connection that ' it is a surprising thing that in regard to the liturgical chant our preferences and our taste accord with those of the Christians of the West in the fifth and sixth centuries. Here is a decisive proof. Certain melodies that, taking shape in these distant times, seem particularly happy were adapted after the manner of " nomoi " from fixed types, and one meets them upon every page of the Antiphonary. It is precisely these melodies that still to-day fall so gratefully on our ears.'

* A simple and familiar example is the ' Benedicamus Domino' for First Vespers on Solemn Feasts.

No one who has lived any time with plainchant will fail to recognize and find himself recalling such delightful signposts as those noted below, which are indeed capable of being put to the most varied use and appear in any of the modes, being atonal.

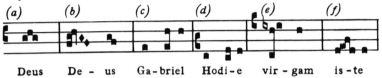

We meet also, for the avoidance of monotony, as Dom Gatard points out in his monograph on the chant, ' with contrary motion, repetitions, imitations, melodic echoes, musical rhymes, and (in a word) all that is necessary to make the Gregorian chant pleasing and artistic so long as it remains within the bounds of what is sufficiently restrained for use in worship*'.

Now in addition to the recognition of these formulas, helpful in the matter of coherent interpretation of the music, we should, to develop the power of, and to improve, phrasing, be alert to appreciate the forms, or patterns, in which pieces of plainchant are cast; and this may be done without emulating the dissecting chamber methods of the Solesmes scriptorium, valuable for the student as these are. It should be a matter of little surprise, when one realizes the deep-rooted nature of the basis of all artistic principles, that the chant contains the seeds of all the forms used in modern music. Not only binary and ternary forms, simple and developed, the rondo, and incipient sonata form, but, if it may be put under this heading, a hint of the *arioso* style that Bach in his Passions and Church Cantatas was to bring to such a pitch of perfection.

The swing to and fro of the melodic line should be felt even in so very simple an example as the following exhortation:

(Let us proceed in peace. In the name of Christ. Amen.)

Cantors and choir should feel something of the pleasure of the tight-rope walker's balance in poising their versicles and responses!

Plainchant, by Dom Gatard, p. 20. Church Music Monographs, No. 4. (Faith Press.)

℣. Réges Thársis et ín - sulae   múne - ra óf - fe - rent.

℞. Réges   A - rabum et   Sá - ba   dó - na   ad - dú - cent.

(The kings of Tharsis and the island shall offer gifts. The kings of
Arabia and Saba shall bring presents.)

The Compline response (as also the responses at Prime and the Little
Hours) takes to itself the exact form of a rondo. The plan is:

    A. Soloist. *In manus tuas Domine commendo spiritum meum.*
    A¹. Chorus. *In manus tuas Domine commendo spiritum meum.*
    B. Soloist. *Redemisti nos Domine.*
    A². Chorus. *Commendo spiritum meum.*
    C. Soloist. *Gloria Patri et Filio et Spiritui Sancto.*
    A³. Chorus. *In manus tuas*, etc.

6

In manus tu - as Dó - mi - ne, * Comméndo spí - ri - tum meum.

In manus. ℣. Re - de - místi   nos Dó - mi - ne,   De - us ve -

- ri - tá - tis. * Comméndo. ℣. Glori - a   Pa - tri, et Fí - li - o,

et Spirí - tu - i Sancto.   In manus.

(Into Thy hands, O Lord, I commend my spirit. Into Thy hands,
Thou hast redeemed us, O Lord, God of truth. I commend. Glory be
to the Father, and to the Son, and to the Holy Spirit. Into Thy hands.)

Phrase balances with phrase in direct contrast in these simple examples of binary and ternary form: and a search through the *Antiphonale* and the *Graduale* will show a wonderful variety of treatment in phrase-balancing.

5.a

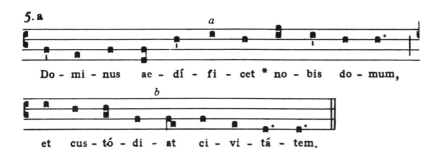

Do - mi - nus   ae - dí - fi - cet * no - bis   do - mum,

et   cus - tó - di - at   ci - vi - tá - tem.

(Let the Lord build our house, and guard our city.)

Off. *Vir erat*

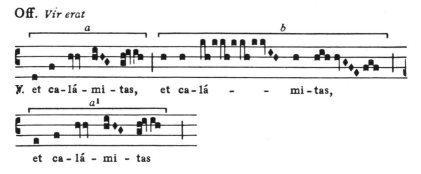

℣. et ca-lá - mi - tas,   et ca-lá   -   -   mi - tas,

et   ca - lá - mi - tas

(And calamity.)

Sometimes the phrases of contrast are long delayed, as in these two lovely motets:

6

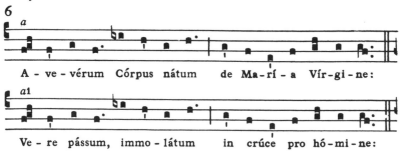

A - ve - vérum Córpus nátum   de Ma-rí - a Vír-gi-ne:

Ve - re pássum, immo - látum   in crúce pro hó - mi - ne:

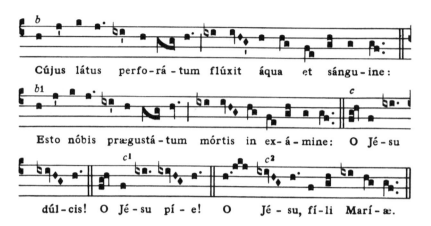

Cújus látus perfo-rá-tum flúxit áqua et sángu-ine:

Esto nóbis præ gustá-tum mórtis in ex-á-mine: O Jé-su

dúl-cis! O Jé-su pí-e! O Jé-su, fí-li Marí-æ.

(Hail, true Body, born of the Virgin Mary: truly suffering, sacrificed on the Cross for man: Whose pierced side flowed with water and blood: Forearm us in the trial of death. O sweet Jesus! O loving Jesus! O Jesus, Son of Mary!)

6

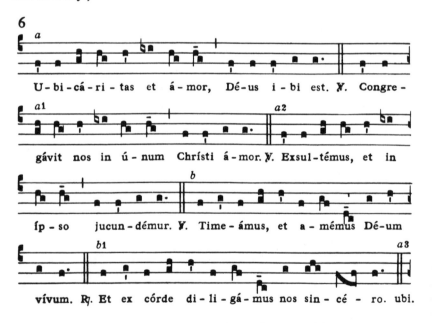

U-bi-cá-ri-tas et á-mor, Dé-us i-bi est. ℣. Congre-

gávit nos in ú-num Christi á-mor. ℣. Exsul-témus, et in

íp-so jucun-démur. ℣. Time-ámus, et a-mémus Dé-um

vívum. ℞. Et ex córde di-li-gá-mus nos sin-cé-ro. ubi.

(Where is charity and love, there God is. The love of Christ has drawn us together. Let us rejoice, and be glad in Him. Let us fear, and love the living God. And with a sincere heart let us love each other. Where is charity?)

The musical designs of the hymns, which range from the purely syllabic to the fairly ornate, are exquisitely varied and free. The writers never seem to be cramped by the metrical scheme of the poems, but indeed appear to delight in escaping from these bonds.

It is true that a few of the plainchant hymn tunes limp along painfully (e.g., the hymn for the Feast of the Conversion of St Paul), but the majority are fine melodies and deserve to be far better known and used.

Some idea of the variety of design employed may be gathered from a glance at six of the eight settings of ' *Iste Confessor* '.

No. 1. Partial repetition (*a*) and sequences (*b*).

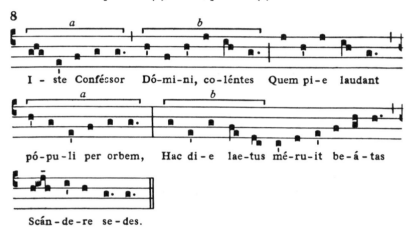

(He is that Confessor of the Lord, whom lovingly the peoples of the whole world honour and praise; on this day was he joyfully found worthy to ascend to the seats of the blessed.)

No. 2. (The same.) Repetition of the first phrase.

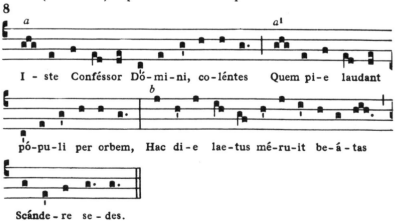

No. 3. (The same.) No repetition except the ' incise ' in the last bar.
8

I - ste Conféssor Dó-mi - ni,   co - léntes   Quem pi - e   laudant

pó-pu-li per orbem, Hac di - e lae - tus mé-ru - it be - á - tas

Scánde - re se - des.

No. 5. (The same.) The phrase at ' *hac die* ' has an affinity with that at ' *Iste Confessor Domini Colentes* '. This is a particularly fine tune.
2

I - ste Conféssor Dó-mi - ni, co - léntes Quem pi - e láudant

pó-pu-li per órbem, Hac dí - e laé-tus mé-ru - it be - á - tas

Scán-de - re sé - des.

No. 6. (The same.) An ornate version into which are woven not quite successfully two stock formulas, the first being repeated at the close.
I

I - ste Conféssor Dó-mi-ni, co-léntes Quem pi - e láudant

pó-pu-li per órbem, Hac dí - e laé-tus mé-ru - it be - á - tas

Scán-de - re sé - des.

No. 8. (The same.) In contrast to the above, here is a purely syllabic version with no phrase repetition.

I - ste Conféssor   Dó-mi-ni, co-léntes Quem pi - e láudant

pó-pu - li per órbem, Hac dí - è laé-tus mé-ru - it be-á - tas

Scán-de - re sé - des.

Jesu Corona Virginum. No. 1. This hymn is exquisitely designed. It shows a great feeling for sequence, and is beautifully rounded off by the repetition, at the last line, of the first half-phrase.

Je - su co - ró - na Vírgi - num, Quem Mater il - la cón - ci - pit,

Quae so - la Virgo pár-tu - rit: Haec vo - ta clemens ác-ci - pe.

(Dear crown of all the Virgin choir!
That holy Mother's Virgin Son!
Who is, alone of womankind,
Mother and Virgin both in one.)

No. 2. (The same.) An interesting variation in form. The whole first phrase is immediately repeated.

Je - su co - ró - na Vírgi - num, Quem Mater il - la cón - ci - pit,

Quae so - la Virgo pár-tu - rit: Haec vo - ta clemens ác-ci - pe.

Compare also the five settings of ' *Ave Maris Stella* ' (Feasts of Our Lady) or the five of ' *Deus tuorum Militum* ' (Communion of one Martyr). The attention of a choir should always be directed to the design of a piece of chant it is going to sing. This can be done in a very few words and the mental appreciation of the design is undoubtedly an aid to intelligent phrasing.

In long prose pieces we shall find a formula brought into the music at varying distances such as that at *magnum—mysterium—Domine*: and in many other instances given before. Round these signposts the interpretation is built up.

(The great mystery of His heritage: a womb knowing not a man has been made the temple of God: taking His flesh from her, He was not stained: all the nations shall come, saying: ' Glory to Thee, O Lord.')

We shall often find the pattern of the ' echo ' phrases in other places than in an *Alleluia*. In the Offertory below (Third Sunday after Pentecost), care must be taken by using different degrees of tone at the repetitive phrases to avoid giving the impression of a singing exercise!

quis   quaerén - tes   te :   psál-li - te Dó - mi - no,

qui há - bi - tat   in   Sí - on: quó - ni - am   non

est ob - lí - tus   o - ra - ti - ó - nem páupe - rum.

(Let all hope in Thee, who have known Thy name, O Lord: since thou
dost not desert those who seek Thee: sing praises unto the Lord, Who
lives on Sion: since He has not forgotten the prayer of the poor.)

Always these clues, formulas, leading motives, signposts, should be
diligently sought. They stand out like windmills on the Norfolk flats,
which merge into the landscape, and if carefully emphasized—not over-
emphasized—are excellent means of giving shape and intelligibility to
music that may easily sound entirely formless and as little likely to stop
as a cold-water tap that has been left running.

1. D

Tri-bus mi - rá - cu - lis * or - ná - tum di - em sanctum

có - li - mus: hó - di - e   stella Magos du - xit ad praesé -

- pium: hó - di - e   vinum ex aqua factum est ad núpti - as :

hó - di - e   in Jordá - ne a Jo - ánne Christus bapti - zá - ri vó - lu -

- it,   ut sal - vá - ret nos, al - le - lú - ia.   E u o u a e.

(We keep holy a day graced with three miracles: to-day the Star guided
the Wise Men to the manger: to-day the wine was made from water

at the wedding: to-day it was the will of Christ to be baptized by John in Jordan, that He might save us, alleluia.)

In the above antiphon (Feast of the Epiphany) the eye will seize at once on the groups at ' *Miraculis* ' and ' *(sanc)tum colimus* '. These are secondary. The signpost of greater importance is the little one at the ' *hodies* '. There is a lovely balance between these three—notice that the middle one falls one note to the interval of a fourth—and if the antiphon has been well sung, with a fraction of a pause after each ' *hodie* ', there should stay in the hearer's mind the phrase ' *Tribus miraculis* ' with its three pendant miracles each led up to by a ' *hodie* '.

The key-word may receive a different setting each time as in the case of the three ' *beati* ' in the Communion for All Saints, given below.

(Blessed are the clean of heart, for they shall see God: blessed are the peace-makers, for they shall be called the children of God: blessed are they that suffer persecution for justice sake, for theirs is the kingdom of heaven.)

Much more difficult to interpret is the Tract ' *Qui seminant in lacrimis* ' (Common of Many Martyrs).

(They who sow in tears, shall reap in joy. They went their way, and wept, sowing their seed. But coming they shall come with exultation, bearing their sheaves.)

No piece of plainchant could more clearly show the necessity for a careful scrutiny of the text before the music is looked at. The words alternate sorrow and joy: ' *lacrimis* ', ' *gaudio* ', ' *flebant* ', ' *exsultatione* '.

Examining the music, we find the one permitted accidental, B♭, prominent in the ' *lacrimis* ' group, but it is the fivefold repetition of the ' C ' which characterizes ' *gaudio mitent* ', a cry of joy, and at the cadence the B♭ is corrected. At the start of the versicle the sad B♭s of ' *lacrimis* ' still a little overshadow the music, and we have not yet reached the final

joy of '*exsultatione*', when they have quite disappeared. The passage
from grief to gladness needs the highest degree of vocal control. Any
choir who can successfully tackle this Tract may next turn its attention
to the wonderfully subtle and exquisitely tender antiphon depicting
the anointing of Our Lord's feet by St Mary Magdalen, '*In diebus illis*',
noting the related neumatic groups at *peccatrix, leprosi, ejus: cognovit,
capillis: alabastrum, unguento:* and the expressive figure attached to
lacrimis.

7. a

In di - é - bus il - lis,* mú-li - er quae e - rat in ci - vi - tá - te

peccátrix,   ut cognó - vit quod Jesus ac-cú-bu-it   in domo

Simó-nis le-pró-si, át-tu - lit a - la-bá - strum un -

guénti: et stans re-tro   se-cus pe-des Dó-mi-ni Je-su,

lá - crimis coepit ri-gá-re pédes e - jus,   et ca-píl - lis

cá-pi-tis su i ter-gé-bat: et os-cu-la-bá - tur pedes

e - jus,   et un-guén-to un-gé-bat   E u o u a e.

(In those days, a woman who was in the city, a sinner, when she knew
that Jesus had sat down in the house of Simon the leper, brought an

alabaster box of ointment: and standing behind at the feet of the Lord Jesus, she began to sprinkle His feet with tears, and wiped them with her hair: and kissed His feet, and anointed them with ointment.)

Another very striking piece is the Offertory for the Feast of St Michael, in which one solemn low-pitched little phrase (*a*), twice repeated, gives a hieratic atmosphere to the picture of the swinging golden censer in the angel's hand; while the clouds of incense ascend in the long melismatic phrase given to ' *ascendit* ', the censer itself rising and falling in the neumatic groups at ' *habens thuribulum aureum* '.

(An Angel stood near the altar of the temple, holding a golden censer in his hand: and much incense was given to him: and the smoke of the spices rose up in the sight of God, alleluia.)

CHAPTER VIII

PLAINCHANT AND BYZANTINE ART

Analogy is no substitute for interpretation, and comparisons between one art and another are notoriously misleading, but, nevertheless, encouraged by a pamphlet on ' Architecture and Music ' by Alexander Walton (Heffer, 1935), in which he tries to justify the comparison of two such very different arts as these, one existing in time, the other in space, I want very briefly to throw out some suggestions for the comparison of plainchant with Byzantine art and architecture*.

This comparison is suggested in Cecil Gray's brilliant chapter on ' Gregorian Music ' in his *History of Music*. He rightly says there that the Greek and Hebrew origins of the chant have all too easily been taken for granted and on very slender evidence. It is the nature of Greek music, as far as we know anything about it, to be cold and dry, whereas Gregorian Chant ' is the very opposite of cold and dry, and if not feminine exactly, is certainly romantic—in so far as the word has any meaning—and, above all, subjective.' Then the vivid descriptions of Hebrew music in the Old Testament—and it is full of them—describe ' an art brilliant, sensual, and triumphant ', but one radically opposed to ' the spirit of gentleness, humility, and resignation, which is the dominating characteristic of the Gregorian Chant '.

Therefore, in spite of Greek, Hebraic, and other elements present in the chant, ' we shall almost certainly be right if we agree to regard the Liturgical chant of the Catholic Church as neither Greek nor Hebrew, nor even as a combination of both, but an entirely new form of musical art corresponding to the Church of *Hagia Sophia* at Constantinople or the mosaics of Ravenna. It unmistakably reveals not only the same spiritual characteristics, but even the same technical features as all the other forms of Byzantine art. The melodic principle, to which reference

* In the introduction to *Musicians of Former Days* (Kegan Paul), Romain Rolland writes: ' It is perfectly right to give music every possible kind of name; for it is an architecture of sound in certain centuries of architecture and with certain architectural people, such as the Franco-Flemings of the fifteenth and sixteenth centuries. It is also drawing, line, melody, and plastic beauty, with people who have an appreciation and admiration for form, with painter and scupltor people, like the Italians. It is inner poetry, lyrical outpouring, and philosophic meditation, with poets and philosophers like the Germans. It adapts itself to all conditions of society. It is a courtly and poetic art under Francis I and Charles IX; an art of faith and fighting with the Reformation; an art of affectation and princely pride under Louis XIV; an art of the *salon* in the eighteenth century. Then it becomes the lyric expression of revolutionaries; and it will be the voice of the democratic societies of the future, as it was the voice of the aristocratic societies of the past. No formula will hold it. It is the song of centuries and the flower of history; its growth pushes upward from the griefs as well as from the joys of humanity.'

has already been made, of the ascent to descent from a central point—a simple formula which, nevertheless, underlies practically the whole *corpus* of Gregorian Chant—is essentially the musical equivalent of the curved arch and flowing semicircular lines which constitute the dominant structural motive of *Hagia Sophia* and practically all Byzantine architecture; and the inner spirit that informs the liturgical chant is recognizably one with that which finds expression in Byzantine mosaics*.'

Curved arches and semicircular lines may be seen in the interior of Westminster Cathedral, which is Byzantine in inspiration, and certainly in their varying size and rhythmic simplicity do suggest that rise and fall (*arsis* and *thesis*) to which I so often allude in this book.

The ' inner spirit ' of which Mr Gray speaks may also be seen in the best mosaics in Westminster Cathedral or in the Greek Church in Moscow Road, London, W.2—since few of us can visit Ravenna—and declares itself always and everywhere as ' curiously ethereal, static, arrested and timeless '—the artistic expression of the *pneuma* of contemporary Alexandrinian theology

It is probably useless to enlarge upon this excellent description without the aid of illustration, but I can assure the reader that a visit to Ravenna made recently confirmed all that Mr Gray says. The lines of the architecture, the designs of the mosaics, were, if any comparison was to be made, comparable in a special manner, if not exclusively, to plainchant: and a long contemplation of the lovely Byzantine art of this ancient place convinced me, as the study of the music alone never could have, how infinitely important it is to preserve the continuous unbroken flow of the chant throughout a whole rhythmic period (or phrase). It was possible to clothe musically a series of three arches with a *Kyrie* or an *Agnus Dei* (threefold forms), and feel the rhythmic rise and fall of the music along the lines of the arches.

It was easy, also, to compare the designs of syllabic, neumatic, and ornate chants with those of the mosaics, but not so easy—indeed, impossible—to find a parallel in the chant for their exquisite colouring. Pitch in music is said by Mr Walton to correspond to colour, that is, the texture of a note to that of a material, but the colour of the mosaic is a surface texture comparable to the ' colour ' of an orchestral instrument. In regard to the chant, such a ' colour ' can, of course, only be found in the voice which is itself coloured by the vowels and consonants of the words it sings as well as, in some sense, by pitch and volume. The mosaics and the chant are indeed ' timeless ' in the sense of being outside the changing fashions of different ages. They are, essentially, of no age but for all ages. Having resisted secular influences so strongly, and having been so peculiarly the fruit of the religious spirit, they are as little antique or in thrall to convention as is the New Testament.

* *History of Music*, p. 17. Cecil Gray. (Kegan Paul.)

It remains to be seen if Ruskin's description of the characteristics of the School of incrusted architecture, with its chromatic decorations represented by St Mark's, Venice*, finds any parallel in the art of plainchant.

(1) There is no deep cutting.

(1) *There is no intensity of expression. The climatic accent-points are melodic rather than intensive.*

(2) The designs are wrought on a flat surface.

(2) *Psalmody is the flat surface of the chant, and stretches of it appear in the ornate chants as well.*

(3) The ornamental arrangements atone for feebleness of portraiture.

(3) *The chant depends on melodic design for its appeal and forgoes the reinforcements of harmony and counterpoint.*

(4) The sculptures of the incrusted school are generally distinguished by care and purity rather than force.

(4) *Exactly the same may be said of the ' sculpturing ' of the chants.*

(5) The impression of the architecture is not to be dependent on size.

(5) *Plainchant is also independent of size. It does not set out to be imposing, but is an intimate and withdrawn art.*

(6) Byzantine architecture requires expression and interesting decoration over vast plane surfaces, decoration which becomes noble only by becoming pictorial.

(6) *The melodic line of plainchant flows over such surfaces—psalmody with its long dominant reciting note is at the root of nearly all the chant— and becomes noble by means of the vitalizing Word which finds its tonal embodiment in the music.*

(7) All efforts of Byzantine art to represent violent action are inadequate, most of them ludicrously so, even when the sculptural art is in other respects advanced.

(7) *Plainchant is equally unable to represent violence of action (or emotion), at least unless violence is done to it by accent-hammering.*

(8) (Byzantine art) does not bother with anatomy or perspective—its colouring is seldom to be seen in nature; it is not concerned with this world, but with the world of the spirit. Like the Liturgy, it repeats certain well-known forms: Like an oft-seen play of Shakespeare, familiarity only helps us to appreciate it the more†.

(8) *Plainchant is coloured by its modes; European music ever tended towards the tonic and dominant of the two modern scales. Plainchant, as we can see, uses certain formulas over and over again, and of these we never tire.*

I hope this list of parallels will be found not merely ingenious or strained, but genuinely useful and thought-provoking. The reader

* *The Stones of Venice*, Vol. II, Chapter IV. Ruskin. (Dent.)

† This quotation is taken from *Byzantine Art*, p. 116. Rice. (Clarendon Press, 1935.)

who is interested in the comparison may easily obtain photographs and postcards (some in not too bad colour) of the churches and mosaics at Ravenna and of St Mark's, Venice, at small cost, from Mr Mansell, Elfin Works, Hanwell, Middlesex.

I particularly recommend as an example of beautiful design and rhythm the dance (for so it appears) of the four Apostles in the central cupola of St Mark's (Alinari, 3643), ' The Washing of the Feet ' in the same church (Alinari, 32418), and the wonderful design of the ' Creation of the World ' in the vestibule (various photographs). But more valuable than these thirteenth-century mosaics are the ones of the fifth and sixth centuries at Ravenna. The exquisite ' Doves Drinking at a Fountain ' (*Galla Placida*) or ' The Last Supper ' (*S Apolinare Nuovo*) are miracles of design; while in the long line of Virgins offering gifts to Our Lady, culminating in the presentation of the Three Kings, in the same church one may see, without perhaps too great a strain on the imagination, a psalm and its antiphon!

As this is a matter rather to be felt individually than discussed, I give below a list of books in which the interested reader may pursue his researches.

(1) *Byzantine Art.* Rice. (Clarendon Press.)

(2) *The Byzantine Empire.* Norman Baynes. (Home University Library.)

(3) *The Birth of Western Painting.* Robert Byron. (Routledge.)

(4) *La Peinture Byzantine.* Paul Muratoff. (G. Crès.) (With 256 excellent illustrations.)

The last two books are now remaindered cheaply.

CONCLUSION

I reach the end of this book conscious that I have only been able to touch on the fringe of a subject about which little has yet been written, and that I have treated it in a very summary manner.

One criticism, amongst others that may arise, must be met here. The choirmaster will object that comparatively few of the musical examples chosen will come into the ken of the average choir, whose view of plainchant is limited to what is done on Sunday mornings at Mass, and in the happy but far too few places where Sunday Vespers are sung. Many of the examples, therefore, will only be heard where the Liturgy is fully carried out, as at Westminster Cathedral.

To have confined myself to the plainchant of the Sunday Masses and Vespers would have resulted in a text-book of considerable size, practical indeed, and eminently worth doing, but a book differing in character from the original impulse in my mind. It may at least be said that the ideas that emerge in this book are universally applicable, and I have been concerned to give as comprehensive review of the variety of the chant as was compatible with the size of the book, thinking to interest all musicians into whose hands it might come.

We look, indeed, for a widespread revival of the congregational singing of the beautiful Hours of Vespers and Compline—a revival that can only come about when people possess themselves of a service-book such as the little volume of ' Plainsong for Schools ', with the psalms noted, and if they are given intelligent, interesting, and encouraging help— but even then many of my examples fall in the week and not on the Sundays.

I suggest that for the sheer love of the chant and, therefore, of the Liturgy—since it should not be possible to love one and hate the other— study groups should meet from time to time in one another's houses, and sing through, quietly and reflectively, without too much regard for accuracy but every attention to the spirit of the chant, the most attractive examples of the chant that will never have performance in their churches.

If these meetings, perhaps taking place round a table in the manner of the madrigalists, were kept free from too great a concentration on formal analysis or preoccupation with rhythmic problems, especially, and from liturgical aestheticism or fanaticism, but were punctuated by little bouts of discussion, I can imagine that they would be very helpful and inspiring, and do much to hasten the liturgical revival that we all so greatly desire and have at heart.

Finally, it will be well to repeat on this last page the saying of a great Pope:

' *In necessariis unitas, in dubiis libertas, in omnibus caritas.*'

(In essentials unity, in non-essentials liberty, in all things charity.)

'If to the enormous importance of the part which Gregorian chant played in the history, not only of music but of all the arts, we add that which it played in medieval life generally, and consider how, for example, the chant which was used on a particular day would be cited in statutes and chronicles as a means of dating an event; how official ceremonies and public observances of all kinds were celebrated to its solemn and majestic strains; how it accompanied the lives of all, noble and peasant, great and humble, rich and poor, cleric and layman, from the cradle to the grave—then indeed we begin to realize the overwhelming cultural significance of this great Roman fountain of song, as sweet and pure and inexhaustible as the Acqua Virgo of the Eternal City itself, and playing endlessly, day and night, throughout the centuries, like the fountains in the Place of St Peter before the sanctuary which is the heart and core of Christendom.'

History of Music, p. 23. Cecil Gray. (Kegan Paul.)

SELECTED BIBLIOGRAPHY

1. HISTORY OF THE LITURGY.
Christian Worship: Its Origin and Evolution. Monsignor Duchesne.
(S.P.C.K.) (Only obtainable now secondhand.)
The Mass of the Western Rites. Abbot Cabrol. (Sands, 1934.)
The Books of the Latin Liturgy. Abbot Cabrol. (Sands, 1932.)
The Breviary: Its History and Contents. Dom Baudot. (Sands, 1929.)
Liturgical Prayer: Its History and Spirit. Abbot Cabrol. (Burns & Oates.)
The Mind of the Missal. Fr. C. C. Martindale. (Sheed & Ward, 1929.)
The Words of the Missal. Fr. C. C. Martindale. (Sheed & Ward, 1933.)
The Church and the Catholic. Romano Guardini. (Sheed & Ward, 1936.)

2. OFFICE AND MASS BOOKS WITH LATIN AND ENGLISH TEXT.
The Daily Missal. (Cabrol or Lefebure.)
The Day Hours of the Church. (Burns & Oates.)
The Vesperal. (Burns & Oates.)

3. THE HISTORY OF PLAINCHANT.
(A) Books in English.
Religious Music. Rene Agrain. (Sands.)
(The first 111 pages of this book give an excellent account of the matter.)
History of Music. Cecil Gray. (Kegan Paul.)
(The most illuminating and provocative short history of music in English. One chapter is devoted to Gregorian music, a good allowance for a book of this size, and it alone is worth the price of the book.)
Early History of Singing. W. J. Henderson. (Longmans, New York.)
(A valuable account of an important matter. Must be sought for secondhand.)
Plainchant*. Dom Gatard. (Faith Press, 1921.)
Latin Hymnody. Rev. H. V. Hughes. (Faith Press, 1922.)

(B) Books in French.
L'Art Grégorien. Gastoué. (Felix Alcan.)
Les Mélodies Grégoriennes. Dom J. Pothier. (Desclée.)
Origine et développement du Chant Liturgique jusqu'à la fin du Moyen âge. (P. Wagner.)
(Three classics of the Gregorian revival, the value of which new discoveries have not invalidated. The last is a translation from the German. The English edition is hard to find now.)

* The first of these Church Music Monographs is especially to be recommended.

4. TEXT BOOKS.

(A) In English.

A Grammar of Plainsong. A Benedictine of Stanbrook. (Rushworth & Dreaper, third edition, 1934.)
(An excellent and practical book, but weak on the aesthetic side.)
Plainsong. Rev. Thomas Helmore. (Novello.)
(Old-fashioned but thorough. It is addressed primarily to Anglicans.)
The Rudiments of Plainchant. F. Burgess. (Offices of *Musical Opinion*, second edition, 1933.)
(A good short account for Anglicans.)
Catechism of Gregorian Chant. Dom Hugle. (Fischer, 1927.)
(A good book for schools and choirs.)
How to Sing Plain Chant. Fr. J. Harrison, O.P. (St Dominic's Press, 1919.)
(A beautifully printed and excellent book especially addressed to Dominicans)
Text Book of Gregorian Chant According to Solesmes. Dom G. Suñol. (Desclée.)
(A poor translation and a faintly irritating book.)
The Music of the Roman Rite. A Manual for Choirmasters. R. R. Terry. (Burns & Oates, 1931.)
Le Nombre Musical Grégorien, Vol. I. Dom André Mocquereau. (Desclée.)
(A fair translation of a part of the Solesmes classic in which the rhythmic theories of Solesmes are fully exposed.)

(B) In French.

Méthode Pratique de Chant Grégorien. Dom L. David. (Janin, 1922.)
(The best account of the principles of what is loosely called the ' accentualist ' school. It deserves to be read with attention, and the ideas put forward compared with those of Solesmes.)
La Musicalité Grégorien. Dom J. Gajard. (Desclée, 1931.)
(In spite of an unattractive style and a pronounced inferiority complex, this little book by the Choirmaster of Solesmes is worth having, as it deals more with interpretation than with rhythm.)

(C) In Italian.

Canto Gregoriano: Principi Teorici e Pratici. Abbot Ferretti. (Desclée, third edition, 1933.)
Estetica Gregoriano*, Vol. I. (Pontifical Institute of Sacred Music, 1934.)
(An English translation of these two masterly works is badly needed. The first book is the best of all the text-books, clear, sane, and practical: and the second, which covers a wide field, is a treatise on the musical forms of the Gregorian Chant of the greatest value. The Abbot's Italian is easy to read.)

* Vol. II is not yet published.

5. VOCAL WORKS.

(A) Covering all the examples in this book, and with Solesmes rhythmic signs, traditional notation, and Latin text only.

Graduale Romanum. 7s. 6d. (Desclée.)

Vesperale Romanum. 7s. 6d. (Desclée.)

Officium et Missa Ultimi Tridui Majoris. 1s. 8d. (Desclée.)

(The *Liber Usualis*, edited by the Benedictines of Solesmes, should be mentioned here. It is a useful if bulky compendium for general purposes, and contains the Masses and Vespers of all the greater Feasts as well as Sundays, the music of Holy Week, etc., and costs 7s., bound in paper. A similar book in Modern Notation, text in Latin and French, and rhythmic signs designed by the author, is edited by A. Gastoué, and costs only 4s. 6d., bound in cloth. P. Lethelheux, Paris, 1935.)

Chants Abrégés des Graduels, des Alleluias et des Traits. (Desclée.)

(Useful abridgements of these difficult pieces, founded upon ancient psalm formulas.)

(B) Vocal Works without the rhythmic signs of Solesmes.

Graduale Romanum. (Plainsong & Mediaeval Music Society, 1931.)

(The unedited text with the introduction in English.)

Gradual Dominical. (Librairie St Grégoire, 22 Rue du Lycée, Grenoble.)

Vesperal Dominical. (Librairie St Grégoire, 22 Rue du Lycée, Grenoble.)

(Dom David's Grenoble edition puts the square notation on a five-line stave with a ' key-signature '. Only one rhythmic sign is used—that of prolongation. Text in Latin and French. The books cover only Sundays and the Greater Feasts.)

Plainsong for Schools. Two volumes, 6d. each. (Desclée.)

English Translation of the first volume, 6d.

(An excellent selection for congregational use.)

(The reader is advised to send for Messrs Rushworth & Dreaper's admirable Plainchant Catalogue for particulars of many other vocal works, magazines, accompaniments, etc. There are many other versions of the Vatican text issued, such as the beautifully printed volumes of Pustet, in traditional and modern notation, but they are at present very expensive. I especially wish to recommend *Music and Liturgy*, the organ of the Society of St Gregory, as a magazine of much interest to the lover of plainchant.)

(C) Anglican Vocal Works:

Order of Vespers.

Ordinary of the Mass.

Book of Introits.

A Selection of Grails, Alleluias, and Tracts.

(Dr Palmer's adaptations from the Sarum Books. St Mary's Convent, Wantage.)

A Holy Week Book. (The Plainsong & Mediaeval Music Society.)

(For other publications, see the catalogue of this Society.)

6. BOOKS OF GENERAL INTEREST.

J. S. Bach. 2 vols. Albert Schweitzer. (Black.)
(Ernest Newman's translation of this wonderful book.)
Collected Essays—XXI-XXVI. Robert Bridges. (Oxford Press.)
(Dealing with the Liturgy of the Anglican Church, these essays
contain much of interest to the musician of any creed.)
Interpretation in Song. Plunket Greene. (Macmillan.)
(No choirmaster should be without this book.)
Music and Worship. Walford Davies and Harvey Grace. (Eyre &
Spottiswoode.)
The Training of Catholic Choirs. D. J. Edeson. (Cary.)
L'Eglise et la Musique. A. Gastoué. (Grasset.)
(An excellent little book. About 3s. 6d.)
Introductory Volume to the Oxford History of Music. (Oxford Press.)
The Approach to Plainsong through the Office Hymn. J. H. Arnold,
2s. 6d. (Oxford Press.)

INDEX OF COMPLETE MUSICAL EXAMPLES

ALLELUIA VERSES

	Page
Angelus Domini	82
De profundis	52
Flores	71
Oportebat	39
Stabat Sancta Maria	85
Vidimus stellam	47
Vox turturis	71

ANTIPHONS

Ad Jesum	59
Amen, amen, dico vobis	58
Beata Agnes	82
Dedisti Domine	61
Dixit Mater Jesus	68
Dominus aedificet	93
Dominus veniet	59
Ego plantavi	80
Fulcite me floribus	57
Hodie	61
In diebus illis	102
Joannes et Paulus	57
Laudemus Dominum	25
Magnum haereditatis	98
Magi videntes stellam	69
Mitte manum	36
Nativitas tua	60
O Doctor	38
O sapientia	38
Pastores venerunt	82
Puellae saltanti	57
Qui vult	58
Quod uni	56
Spiritus qui a Patre	36
Stans autem Jesus	66
Tribus miraculis	99
Tu es pastor	56
Videntes stellam	28
Virgo prudentissima	60

COMMUNIONS

Amen dico vobis quidquid	54
Beati mundo corde	100
Dicit Dominus	72
Ecce Virgo	36
Jerusalem surge	80

	Page
Lutum fecit	24
Passer invenit	87
Pater, si non potest	35
Petite	88
Qui manducat	68
Videns Dominus	70
Vidimus stellam	49
Vox in Rama	69

GRADUALS

Liberasti nos	51
Omnes de Saba	46
Timebunt gentes	85

HYMNS

Ave Maris Stella	37
Iste Confessor	95, 96, 97
Jesu Corona Virginum	97
Omnis expertam	31
Pange lingua gloriosi	22
Te lucis	23

INTROITS

Dicit Dominus	50
Ecce advenit	45

OFFERTORIES

Angelus Domini	86
De profundis	53
Reges Tharsis	48
Sperent in te	98
Stetit Angelus	103
Super flumina	87
Tollite portas	81
Vir erat (versicle only: et calamitas)	93

SEQUENCE

Victimae paschali	32

TRACT

Qui Seminant	101

VARIA

Anima Christi	37
Ave verum corpus	93
Ubi caritas	94

GENERAL INDEX

Abbot Aeldred, 42
Abridged Chants, 44
Accents, 26
Accidentals, 10
Agnus Dei, 49, 54
Agrain, 55
Alleluia, 47, 52
Antiphonia, 1
Antiphons, 29, 55
Asterisk, 29, 50
Ave verum corpus, 8

Bach, 3, 18, 19, 76, 91
Beethoven, 35
Benedict XIV, 95
Benedict XV, 41
Benedicite, 4
Bewerunge, 6
Binary, 16
Bistropha, 11
Blackfriars, 1, 8
Brahms, 39
Bridges, Robert, 43
Byzantine Art, 104

Cabrol, 44
Canto Gregoriano, 32
Cantor, 53
Catholic Encyclopedia, 29
Clefs, 10
Climacus, 13
Climax, 34
Clivis, 12, 13, 14
Communion, 49, 54
Compline, 92
Credo, 53

Daily Missal, 44
De Selincourt, Basil, 2
Didron, 55
Dies Irae, 8
Dramatic Dialogue, 63
Dream of Gerontius, 6

Elgar, 6
Eliot, T. S., 2
Epiphany, 44, 100
Erasmus, 74
Estetica Gregoriana, 26, 55
Evolution of Music, 30

Ferretti, 26, 31, 32, 43, 55
Fitzpatrick, 34
FitzWilliam, Virginal Book, 41
Forerunners of Italian Opera, 63
Form, 90
Fourth Council of Carthage, 41
Franck, 19

Gajard, Dom, 7, 90
Garland, 3
Gastoué, 42
Gatard, 91
Gevaert, 90
Gill, 5
Glyn, 30
Gradual, 46, 51, 74, 93
Gray, Cecil, 30, 104
Gregorian Chant, 41, 63, 91, 104
Gregorian Composers, 7, 55, 74, 75, 90
Grenoble, 6, 10, 21
Guardini, 3, 4, 64
Guido of Arezzo, 42

Hagia Sophia, 104
Helmore, 21
Henderson, 2, 42, 63
Hermos, 55
Herwegen, 65
Hin han, 63
Hopkins, Gerald Manley, 2
Hucbald, 41
Hügel, Von, 3
Hymns and Sequences, 30

Ictus, 19, 20
Iste Confessor, 8, 30, 95, 96

Kelly, 1

Lee, Vernon, 63
Lefebure, 44, 49
Liturgy, 64, 65

Magnificat, 27, 29
Manichaeism, 9
Mass in B minor, 19
Melodic Echo, 39
Methode Pratique, 20
Miracle, 64
Moequercan, 16, 56
Motives, 77, 79, 83, 85
Motu Proprio, 1, 6, 41
Moussorgsky, 75
Murray, 16, 25
Music and Liturgy, 73

Neums, 11, 14, 19
Newman, Ernest, 55, 74
Notation, 10

Observer, 2
Offertory, 40, 48, 53, 103
Opus Dei, 4

Painter, Guide, 55
Parry, 3
Parsifal, 64
Pater Noster, 17
Patmore, 4
Pentecost, 49
Phrasing, 23
Podatus, 12, 13, 14
Pomponius Festus, 42
Porrectus, 13
Portamento, 42
Pressus, 14
Psalms, 29
Punctum, 11, 14

Quilisma, 11, 14
Quinquagesima, 66

Ravenna, 104
Rhythm, 15
Rimsky-Korsakoff, 79
Ruskin, 2, 106

Sacra Rapresentazione, 64
Saint Augustine, 2, 4, 8, 43
Saint Bernard, 2, 42
Saint Jerome, 2
Salicus, 13
Scandicus, 12, 13, 14
Scholae Cantorum, 1, 42
Schubert, 25, 75
Schweitzer, 19, 76, 79
Sequence, 31
Short, 55
Sibelius, 55
Solesmes, 5, 6, 7, 15, 19, 20, 21, 36
Spinozism, 9
Stave, 10
Strophicus, 11, 15

Tempo, 35
Tenebrae factae sunt, 8
Ternary, 16
Torculus, 13, 14
Trill, 42
Tristropha, 12

Vatican Gradual, 6
Vespers, 76
Virga, 11
Vonier, 65

Walton, 104
Wellesz, 75
Wolf, 25, 34, 74

Young, 63